Istoria Usolecea 5$

READING CLASSICS

Series Editor

PAOLO BERTINETT

Dean of Faculty of Modern L
and Professor of English Literature,
University of Turin

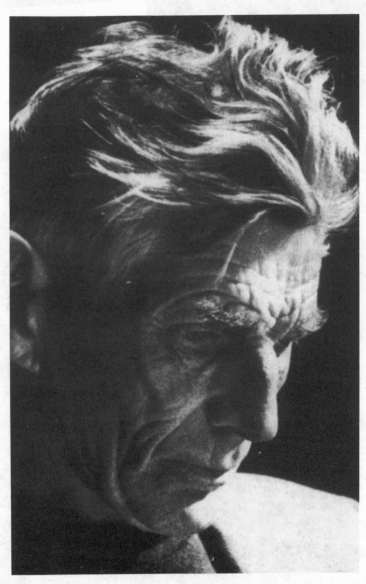

Samuel Beckett in Berlin.

Waiting for Godot

A Tragicomedy in Two Acts

Samuel Beckett

Introduction by

PAOLO BERTINETTI - *University of Turin*

Activities and notes by

BRIAN HODGKISS - *Turin Polytechnic*

© 1952 Les Éditions de Minuit
Selection, introduction, notes and activities
© 1999 Cideb Editrice, Genoa

Front cover illustration by Gianni De Conno

The photographs have been reproduced courtesy of
Les Éditions de Minuit – Archives Samuel Beckett.

We have made every effort to publish this book free of errors.
Please let us know if you notice any we have overlooked.
We would also be happy to receive your comments and suggestions,
and give you other information concerning our material.

We would be happy to receive your comments and suggestions,
and give you any other information concerning our material.
editorial@blackcat-cideb.com
www.blackcat-cideb.com
www.cideb.it

CISQ CISQ CERT
TEXTBOOKS AND
TEACHING MATERIALS
The quality of the publisher's
design, production and sales processes has
been certified to the standard of
UNI EN ISO 9001

Black Cat Publishing is an imprint of Cideb Editrice.

ISBN 978-88-7754-653-1   Book
ISBN 978-88-7754-418-6   Book + CD

Printed in Italy by Litoprint, Genoa

CONTENTS

Introduction   VII

Select Bibliography   XXIII

Chronology   XXXIV

Phonetic Symbols   XLVI

Waiting for Godot   1

Pre-reading Questions   2

Act I   3

Comprehension Questions   68

Act II   87

Comprehension Questions   140

Post-reading Questions   148

Characterisation   159

Structure and Theatrical Technique   163

Language, Style and Symbolism   169

General Questions   172

INTRODUCTION

Samuel Beckett's Achievement

Samuel Beckett did not wish his biography to be written: he considered that only his works, not his life, mattered. Although in a sense, of course, he was right, nevertheless, since some biographical details are useful in evaluating the works, the reader will find a detailed chronology below. This Introduction, on the other hand, will deal only with his theatrical work, though a few brief comments on his life will be helpful.

Beckett was born in Dublin in 1906 into a well-to-do protestant family. He graduated at the University of Dublin where he studied French literature. After obtaining and immediately leaving a teaching post at the University of Dublin, he devoted himself to writing, living mainly in Paris. The author he most admired was James Joyce, whose influence was evident in his first short stories and to some extent also in his first novel, Murphy.

In 1945, at the end of the war, Beckett decided to settle permanently in Paris and to adopt French as his literary language. For many years he wrote only in French, which he himself then translated into English. It was only after some years that he returned, particularly in his theatrical works, to the use of English. The years from 1946 to 1951 were a period of intense creativity, of total dedication to his writing.

His most famous work, the one on which his reputation most depends, was written in the space of a few months, from October 1948 to January 1949. This was a pause, one could say, during the writing of his trilogy of novels, immediately after the completion of *Malone Dies*, his most beautiful narrative work and one of the absolute peaks of the twentieth-century novel. In only two years

Beckett gave to the literature of our time two works of the highest value which, like few others, succeeded fully in expressing its utter anguish and bewilderment.

Of the originality and innovative richness of his exploration of the form of the novel Beckett was fully conscious but not, apparently, at least for a long time, of the even greater originality of his theatrical explorations. Beckett's statements on this subject are well-known. Godot was written 'as a relaxation, to get away from the awful prose [he] was writing at that time.' The theatre was 'a way of distracting [himself] from work on the novel', providing a form which gave 'a defined space' in which people move. There is a statement by Beckett, made in Berlin in November 1967 during the rehearsals of *Endgame*, which gives profound significance to the concept of 'defined space': he sensed the possibility of discovering in the theatre the form most suited to the possibilities of artistic expression in our age (while the novel, at least in the experience of modernist writers, would seem incapable of providing a global and unified vision of reality).

The value of the theatre, says Beckett, lies in the fact that the author creates a little world, with its own laws, and directs the action as on a chess-board. In contrast with the chaos of the world, not reproducible and not knowable, the artist creates his minute, ordered, limited universe, the laws of which he knows because it is he himself who establishes them; and within that universe he controls the characters and their actions. The elimination of the explicit or implicit presence of the author (which in contrast is essential in the novel), the spatial and temporal limitations of theatrical form and the formal obligations which this imposes are paradoxically transformed into the opportunity for freedom. According to Beckett the theatre offers the writer the possibility of expressing himself without the restrictions dictated by 'things' (by the reality external to the artist who creates) and of inventing a world in which he is absolute ruler.

The writing of *Godot*, although it was, as Beckett tells us, dictated by the need to escape from the 'terrible prose' of the *Trilogy*, also arose from the desire to try writing again in dramatic form, which Beckett had occasionally already attempted. After *Le Kid*, an 'irreverent parody' of scenes from Corneille's *Le Cid*, staged in Dublin in 1931, and *Human Wishes*, a play about Dr Johnson, begun in 1937 and abandoned after the writing of the first scene, Beckett, during the period in which he was already working on the *Trilogy*, had written *Eleuthéria*, a play in three acts.

If *Le Kid* was a parody, if the single scene of *Human Wishes* already signalled the unusability of traditional dramatic form, *Eleuthéria* represented a sophisticated and tongue-in-cheek mockery of the complete Western dramatic tradition. Sophocles and Shakespeare, Corneille and Molière, Zola and Shaw, Ibsen and Hauptmann, Yeats and Pirandello were all, at various times, objects of Beckett's derision, but the principal targets for his criticism were naturalistic theatrical conventions. Two sets appeared simultaneously on the stage, the small room of the principal character, Victor, and the drawing-room of the Krapp family (the usual, inevitable drawing-room of late nineteenth and early twentieth century theatre). The whole was placed on a revolving platform and during the third act the 'revolution' of the platform was completed, so that the drawing-room totally disappeared. The obligatory drawing-room of bourgeois theatre was physically removed from the stage. The title *Eleuthéria*, which means 'freedom' in Greek, alludes to Victor's need to free himself from his family, which tries in every way possible to persuade him to return home, and to his winning of the freedom 'to do nothing'; but it also alludes to Beckett's need to free himself from the rules of drama, from the dominant conventions of traditional twentieth century theatre.

The affirmation of the necessity for new forms by parodying those he wished to dispense with was a technique Beckett had already used in fiction in his first delightful novel, *Murphy*, which systematically parodied precisely those narrative techniques of the nineteenth-century novel which modernism had abandoned. Just as *Murphy* (which nevertheless has its own exceptional literary value, beyond its parodic intentions) sweeps away the 'litter' of tradition and foreshadows the novelistic techniques of the *Trilogy*, so *Eleuthéria*, still too limited, however, by the needs of parody, sweeps naturalistic conventions off the stage and leaves the ground clear for the astonishing and unexpected flowering of *Waiting for Godot*.

Fundamentally there have been, in the twentieth century, only two new 'ideas of a theatre', both antithetical, although in different ways, to the naturalistic theatre: that of Beckett and that of Brecht. Brecht's epic theatre, which made an appeal to reason and not to the emotions, refused the unthinking use of identification, heightened by the convention of the 'fourth wall' typical of the naturalistic theatre, and established an effect of rational detachment, of alienation, between stage and spectator by means of various dramatic techniques which aimed at destroying theatrical illusion. Brecht believed that only in this way, by means of a text which shows or describes events rather than emotionally evoking them and which thus represents the world as historically conditioned and therefore modifiable, could the theatre interpret the contemporary world.

   Although the path taken by Beckett was completely different, he too considered the only form available to him incapable of representing his aims. Like Brecht, he felt the need to rid himself of naturalistic conventions, once revolutionary in their ability to capture, through the use of a new language, the world of the late nineteenth century, but, as a result of sterile routine, no longer an adequate means of representing a reality totally different from that which they had been conceived to describe. Instead, however, of creating a form (like Brecht's epic theatre) intentionally antithetical to traditional form, Beckett borrowed the form described by Peter Szondi as 'conversation drama', which had dominated the theatre since the late nineteenth century. He proceeded to drain it of its content, first by reducing the conversation to dialogue which, deprived of any meaningful function, became an end in itself, and then by putting the theatrical event on the stage as theatrical event pure and simple, thus deliberately drawing the audience's attention to the theatrical, non-realistic nature of what it is watching.

Godot as a Summary of Beckett's Dramatic Revolution

Godot has been brilliantly described as a play in which 'nothing happens, twice.' Let us nevertheless try to specify 'what happens' in the two acts of the play.

In Act I, the stage is almost bare: a country road, a low mound and a tree. Estragon, sitting on the mound, is trying to take off his boot; enter Vladimir. The two are waiting for a certain Godot, who seems to have made an appointment with them in that place; while waiting, *they pass the time* talking. Pozzo and Lucky arrive, breaking the monotony of the wait. The former holds the latter on a lead, bullies him and treats him as a slave. Before leaving, Pozzo, wishing to show Vladimir and Estragon, 'who are having such a dull, dull time', proper gratitude for their civility by making Lucky perform, first orders him to dance and then 'to think'. Lucky hurls himself into a speech which becomes more and more confused and hysterical (but of which the subject is nothing less than the contrast between the idea that man has of a loving God and recognition of the sufferings which man must undergo). The speech finishes suddenly when Vladimir succeeds in removing Lucky's hat. After the departure of the slave-master couple, the waiting and the conversation between Vladimir and Estragon continues until the arrival of a boy who informs them that Godot will not come that day but will definitely come the following day.

Act II: the following day. This time Vladimir appears first and then Estragon; their conversation continues; Lucky and Pozzo

reappear (Pozzo has become blind and Lucky dumb); the boy enters
again. Mr Godot will not come that evening but will definitely
come, 'without fail', the following day. The second act ends with the
same words as the first but with the characters reversed. Act I:
'Estragon: Well, shall we go? – Vladimir: Yes, let's go. *They do not
move.*' Act II: 'Vladimir: Well? Shall we go? – Estragon: Yes, let's go.
They do not move.'

It has already been said that Beckett takes the traditional form of
'conversation drama' and completely empties it of meaning.
Practically the whole drama in *Waiting for Godot* consists of
conversation: the dialogue never leads to action and is interrupted
by small scenes which resemble music-hall routines. But the talk
seems like a conversational vacuum, a succession of phrases and
sentences to pass the time, to mitigate the agony of waiting, which
is the essence of the play itself. The two characters wait, and fill the
vacuum of waiting – and of life – by means of conversation which is
in continual need of finding a reason, a pretext for continuing, and
which continually comes to a halt with the central question: the
waiting for Godot. As already stated, there is no real action but
there is a miraculous harmony between form and content.
Theatregoers, faced with a play with the act of waiting at its centre,
recognise themselves in that waiting: waiting for someone who will
not come becomes the form through which the meaning of human
existence is revealed. This does not mean that *Godot* has a
philosophical or metaphysical content that conforms to some
ideological stance. Existentialism, often called upon as a key to a
reading of Beckett's work, is, like other philosophical positions
alluded to in the text, only one of the cultural rationalisations of
which Beckett makes fun. Neither here nor in the works that
followed does his theatre ever suggest interpretations (and even less
messages), but entrusts his *meditations* on the human condition to
the stage – here to four characters, without a history and outside
history, and to their waiting. The other conclusive way in which
Beckett turns the conventions of traditional dramatic form upside

down is provided by metatheatrical moments. In the narrative works, in the *Trilogy* in particular, Beckett often resorts to metanovelistic techniques, which reveal the fictional nature of the narrative text itself. In *Waiting for Godot* Beckett forces the spectator to recognise that he or she is in a theatre, where the actors must speak to justify their own and others' presence. Vladimir asks Estragon to keep the cues going; the two 'pass the ball', commenting on their own words and behaviour from the viewpoint both of the characters and of the actors performing roles before an audience. Theatrical pretence is revealed as pretence; and conversation, in contrast to the dominant role it had in traditional theatre, becomes an empty succession of jokes or witticisms which help to pass the time of waiting and the time it takes to perform the play. Repeatedly the characters behave like actors who perform their routines: Pozzo, for example, after a poetic/philosophic tirade, asks if he was good, apologises for weakening a little towards the end, seeks approval of his performance from his two spectators and hence, by implication, from the audience in general; over-riding the dramatic personages, the actors present themselves *as* actors.

The play is full of comic routines which derive directly from the music-hall and, like the bowler hats which the four characters wear, from comics of silent films such as Charlie Chaplin and Laurel and Hardy. Although this is an essential aspect of a work full of overtly comic moments, the comedy also assumes grotesque connotations which are indissolubly bound up with the tragic nature of the situation. It hardly matters if the audience laughs, because, as Beckett wrote to the director of the first production, 'Nothing is more grotesque than the tragic,' a statement in the same spirit as a remark by Nell, a character in Beckett's next stage play, *Endgame*, who calmly declares that 'nothing is funnier than unhappiness'. Martin Esslin argues that this is the dianoetic laugh, the *risus purus*, as a character in *Watt* says. If we laugh at the characters, we do not laugh derisively; we laugh at human unhappiness in the way we laugh at the most disastrous practical joke of which humanity is victim, the fact that, in the last resort, it is not possible to find any meaning, any aim or any purpose in our existence.

In Beckett can be found explicit echoes of Leopardi and Schopenhauer. On the one hand there is an awareness of the 'infinite vanity of everything'; on the other is the belief that life is a punishment for the original sin of being born. For Beckett's characters, as for Ungaretti's 'creature', 'death is expiated by living'. This is the main thread in all Beckett's work, the principle which presides over the creation of both his theatrical and his fictional characters.

Birth does not represent an entry into life, but an exit, an expulsion from a state of being far preferable to earthly existence. It is an original sin not in the Christian but in the Schopenhauerian sense; and Schopenhauer had already quoted the comment of Calderón De La Barca which Beckett also quotes in his essay on Proust:

> 'Pues el delito mayor del hombre es haber nacido' –
> 'So man's greatest crime is having been born'.
> (*Proust*, Calder, London, 1965, p.67.)

Starting with the *Trilogy*, Beckett's characters, with few exceptions, are old people, often ill and decrepit, who have been expiating through all the long years of their existence 'the sin of being born' and who are by now close to the moment of their death. Death, nevertheless, never seems to arrive – it is 'a long term business'. The annihilation of self is a liberation which, except for the characters of the first narrative works, Beckett's heroes seem not to experience. Almost all are near the end (Molloy and Malone in the *Trilogy*, Hamm, Nagg, and Nell in *Endgame*, Winnie and Willy in *Happy Days*, Krapp, the nameless narrators in *Texts for Nothing*, the characters of the narrative and theatrical texts of the last twenty years), but the end is not reached except that the curtain closes or the book finishes.

In Beckett, however, the idea of a human condition marked by suffering and by the absence of the sense of life itself – an idea so pessimistic that many find it intolerable – remains basic. Such pessimism explains the unease and even rejection that his work aroused in some critics but also explains the unreserved admiration of T.W. Adorno, who found in the work of Beckett a perfect confirmation of his belief that the contemporary work of art can do no other than assert the negativity of the present and reveal its positivity precisely in its affirmation of the negative, which implies the necessity for a Utopian 'other' world. In recent critical work a desire has been shown to redefine the nature of Beckett's pessimism and there has also been a particular insistence on the fact that Beckett's negativity, especially taking into account his personal behaviour, constitutes an antidote to the cynicism, the materialism and the greed of our age. In a world preoccupied solely with money and success at whatever cost, desirous only of being confirmed in its own vulgar and egotistic certainties, Beckettian negation forces us in some way to begin again from zero, to think again, in the light of his secular spirituality, about the sense – or better, the absence of sense – of the world in which we live.

These observations arise from the way in which Beckett brings together the comic and the tragic, a striking example of which occurs in the final scene of *Godot*. Estragon says to Vladimir: 'Why don't we hang ourselves?', at which point he unties the cord that holds his trousers up and they fall down around his ankles. The two pull the cord to test its strength, but the cord breaks, almost making the two men fall. Estragon, as in a music-hall routine, stands, without realising it, only in his underpants, forgetting that his trousers have fallen down. At this point there comes a last comic routine, no longer situational but verbal. 'Vladimir: Pull on your trousers. – Estragon: You want me to pull off my trousers? – Vladimir: Pull ON your trousers.' The tragic nature of the situation, the decision to take their own lives, is incorporated in an inspired moment of pure comedy, which, because there is 'nothing to be done' but laugh at the practical joke of which humanity is victim, continues even when the feasibility of suicide, though not the despair which gave rise to the desire for suicide, recedes.

This scene is also interesting, however, for another reason. The routine, as has been said, is typical of the music-hall. Vladimir and Estragon's appearance, clothes and boots derive from the circus clown, the bowler hats derive from silent films, and Vladimir and Estragon's 'number' in the middle of the second act, 'three hats for two heads', comes directly from the comic routines of Laurel and Hardy and of the Marx Brothers in their masterpiece, *Duck Soup*. Resorting also to 'borrowings' not very far from those of Brecht, but in a dramatic form apparently similar to that of the traditional theatre, Beckett introduces a further element of perversion of traditional form by means of theatrical techniques which come from popular theatre, that is, from 'low' genres in contrast to the 'high' genre of bourgeois theatre.

With *Godot*, therefore, Beckett's idea of a theatre or at least the point of departure and the basis for his idea of a theatre are already clearly indicated. Its characteristics can be summarised thus:
Godot:

a. puts on the stage the theatrical happening itself, revealing the nature of theatrical presentation;
b. uses 'low', popular theatrical forms within a 'high' genre;
c. reduces conversation to dialogue which is an end in itself, depriving it of its function in terms of meaning.

In this way *Godot* undermines the theatrical form that Beckett borrowed, since in the very act of employing it he affirmed its inadequacy. It was a choice of decisive importance both in its influence on some of the most interesting works of contemporary theatre and for Beckett's own work, where it resulted in a technique, adopted with the same rigorous coherence as that pursued in his narrative works, of constant reduction of the dramatic means, tending towards immobility and silence, towards the impossibility of theatre itself.

The First Production of *Godot*

The script of *Godot* had been offered to various impresarios and directors. The only one to show any interest had been Roger Blin, who directed Strindberg's The *Ghost Sonata* at the Théatre de la Gaité. Beckett had seen the performance and had been favourably impressed both by Blin's direction and by the intimate nature of the theatre. In 'Litérature' (3 July 1953), Blin described his first indirect contact with Beckett: 'Four years ago, at the Gaité in Montparnasse, we performed *The Ghost Sonata* in front of an audience of fifteen people. One evening Beckett came. He returned a second time. But I didn't know. One day Tristan Tzara spoke to me about *En attendant Godot*. I don't remember if it was he or Suzanne Dumesnil who brought me the script. At a first reading I didn't see by any means everything that was in the piece, perhaps I didn't even see much in it. [. . .] Its extraordinary richness only became clear to my colleagues and me during the course of rehearsals.'

Beckett and Blin did not meet until the following year, 1950, and even more time was to pass before *Godot* was put on the stage. The Gaité having closed down because of debts in 1951, Blin made arrangements with the nearby Théatre de Poche to have Godot produced in the summer of 1952, but Sacha Pitoeff's production of *Uncle Vanya*, then being performed at the Poche, was so successful that the theatre decided to extend its run of performances for the summer period, cancelling the arrangements for *Godot*.

The first production of *Godot* took place at the Théatre de Babylone on Boulevard Raspail:

> 'Jean-Marie Serreau, who was directing the Babylone at a loss, accepted the risk of increasing the losses by inviting us [to produce Beckett's *Godot*]. He had told me that he was about to pack everything in and so wanted to finish by doing something beautiful. The Babylone was a warehouse converted into a tiny theatre with a stage four metres deep and six metres

wide and with about two hundred and thirty seats. Jean-Marie had taken it over in 1951 and since then had mounted some very beautiful shows there that few people went to see. And the Godot that nobody wanted was able to go on stage on 5 January 1953. [. . .] After a dozen performances the rumour ran throughout Paris that at 38 Boulevard Raspail something remarkable was happening and every evening all seats were sold. We had to borrow chairs from the café on the corner for late or extra spectators. We continued for six months and we did it again the following season.'

(Statement by Roger Blin reported by Lynda Peskine, in *Revue d'Esthétique*, Special Number, Editions Jean Michel Place. Paris 1990, pp. 159-60).

Blin's direction arose from a dialectical relationship with the silences (even more than with the explanations) of Beckett, who was almost always present at rehearsals. In the article from *Revue d'Esthétique* quoted above (pp. 161-62), Blin reconstructs the essential lines of the production:

'In the text the indications regarding the physical appearance [of Vladimir and Estragon] are non-existent. Beckett himself was not able to describe to me either the characters or their dress. He had said: 'I don't see them, but they wear bowler hats.' He said he couldn't see them, but could hear them, and I myself had no definite idea about what Vladimir and Estragon should be. In recompense I visualised immediately what the relationship between the two should be. But it seemed to me that those two tramps should be physically bound to each other, because their relationship is that of an old couple. [. . .] They need each other, they cannot remain separate for long but they can't stand each other any more. When they are happy, when they find each other again, their embraces are analogous to the diastole and the systole [. . .]. They are physically bound to each other but they separate from each other brutally [. . .].

'In the relationship between Pozzo and Lucky he had seen a class relationship. Their relations seemed to me to be of the slave-master type. Obviously I don't mean that *Godot* was a political piece that dealt directly with such a subject, but it seemed evident to me that Pozzo was a master and Lucky a slave, a little like clowns in a circus. Although he had always vigorously denied it, Beckett had, in fact, described just such a situation. He was displeased with my interpretation, which, in the first version, was made obvious by the characters' costumes: Pozzo was very elegantly dressed and Lucky wore livery. [. . .] Beckett saw Lucky as a porter: this idea seemed to me a little conventional and I preferred the more surrealistic dress of a French lackey, because in working in the theatre I am naturally drawn to the *unusual*, unusual even in formal details. I had worked as a director on the character of Pozzo and when I myself then had to interpret the role as an actor I kept myself within the bounds of an extreme stylisation. But also the other actors. It wasn't possible that only Pozzo should act theatrically, in an exaggerated way, and that the other actors should act in a natural way. And in any case *it isn't possible to act Beckett in a natural way.*'

After *Waiting for Godot*

Godot was written straight off, almost without second thoughts. The gestation of the following play, *Endgame*, was, in contrast, extremely difficult; but the final result was a second masterpiece, more 'inhuman' than Godot which, as Beckett himself said, reflects in a representative way the sense of anguish present in much of the culture of that period. *Endgame* speaks to us of a degraded reality, of a world in which nature no longer exists. A world made sterile and lifeless by a nuclear conflict, thought many. The world of today, argued the German philosopher T.W. Adorno, the world after the Second World War, in which everything was destroyed without our being aware of it: the horrors of the war and of the Nazi camps have made us all survivors. As far as the theatrical form of *Endgame* is concerned we again find all the characteristics present in *Godot*. A first turning point occurs in the following work, *Krapp's Last Tape*: in the first place because it was written directly in English and not in French (after this almost all Beckett's theatrical works were written in English); in the second place because there is no longer any dialogue (only an echo of dialogue in the alternation of the voice of Krapp in the present with his voice recorded thirty years before). From this point Beckett keeps the dramatic form within the constraints of the monologue: that of Krapp, the only character who interacts with a former self, that of Winnie, the principal character of *Happy Days* (the other character, Willie, is not an interlocutor but a listener), that of the three characters in *Play*, who do not speak to each other and whose lines, which alternate in the text, if put in sequence, make three different monologues; and so on in almost all the following theatrical works.

If in *Krapp* dialogue is eliminated, in *Happy Days* Beckett eliminates a second basic element of theatrical form: movement. In the first act, the chief character Winnie is buried to the waist and can move only her head and arms. In the second act she is buried to her neck and totally immobile. In the following works in general there will be no more movement. There will be only voices, which reverberate on an ever more abstract scene.

The significance of *Happy Days* lies in the dreamlike words of Winnie and her physical situation, which visually represents her existential condition. Already in previous works there had been the use of images which rejected realism, like the rope which ties Lucky to Pozzo and indicates the subjection of slave to master or like the two ashbins in which Nagg and Nell, the two old people in *Endgame*, are confined. In *Happy Days* the image of the main character contains the very meaning of the play. From this point the theatre of Beckett arises and develops from the visual image. The audience sees the image which fired his imagination and which he then transposed into theatrical form: the image in which lies the meaning of the play.

After *Happy Days* and the following *Play*, Beckett will create theatrical works constructed around a single image or situation which exhausts its possibilities in a few minutes: the scene is abstract, movement is negated or reduced to a minimum, characters in the traditional sense of the word do not exist. And yet the result has great theatricality, as in his first masterpiece.

If we compare the drafts of Beckett's last theatrical works with those of previous works (except in the case of *Godot*), we see that there has been a meticulous process of cutting. Beckett cuts the philosophical and literary references which underlie the text; he cuts the autobiographical references, the allusions to the lived experiences which provided the idea for the play; and finally he removes from the text anything that might seem superfluous, excises complete lines, cuts a single expression, or a single word. Only what is essential must remain. The peculiarity and the power of Beckett's texts lie in their *essentialness*: everything in them is necessary and can be neither modified nor removed. French and English actors who have acted Beckett have often compared the script on which they were working to a musical score. Beckett's dialogues and monologues are like a piece of music, which certainly must be interpreted, but which absolutely cannot be modified: it is not possible to change its notes (that is the words) without destroying its complex harmony.

Paolo Bertinetti

SELECT BIBLIOGRAPHY

Beckett's Theatre Works

The plays are listed in order of composition. First the title of the work is given in the language in which it was originally written (either French or English), then that of Beckett's translation into English or French, then that of the Italian translation. Only the place and date of the first publication of each work are indicated, since all Beckett's theatrical works were published by Éditions de Minuit in France, by Faber and Faber in England and by Einaudi in Italy.

HUMAN WISHES, written in 1937, published in *Disjecta*, Calder, London 1983; *Desideri umani*, EGEA, Milano 1991 (in *Disiecta*, tr. by A. Tagliaferri).

ELEUTHÉRIA, written in 1947, published in 1995 by Éditions de Minuit, Paris, and by Foxrock, Inc., New York (tr. by M. Brodsky).

EN ATTENDANT GODOT, Éditions de Minuit, Paris 1952; *Waiting for Godot*, Grove Press, New York 1954; *Aspettando Godot*, in Samuel Beckett, *Teatro*, Einaudi, Torino 1961, tr. by C. Fruttero [hereafter *Teatro*].

FIN DE PARTIE, Éditions de Minuit, Paris, 1957; *Endgame*, Grove Press, New York, 1978; *Finale di partita* (in *Teatro*).

ALL THAT FALL, Faber, London 1957; *Tous ceux qui tombent*, in 'Les Lettres Nouvelles', mars 1957, tr. by Robert Pinget; *Tutti quelli che cadono* (in *Teatro*).

ACTE SANS PAROLES I, Éditions de Minuit, Paris 1957; *Act Without Words I*, Grove Press, New York 1958; *Atto senza parole* (in *Teatro*).

ACTE SANS PAROLES II, Éditions de Minuit, Paris 1966; *Act Without Words II*, in 'New Departures', 1 (Summer 1959); *Atto senza parole II* (in *Teatro*).

KRAPP'S LAST TAPE, in 'Evergreen Review', vol. 2, n. 5, Summer 1958; *La dernière bande*, in 'Les Lettres Nouvelles', n. 1, 4 mars 1959, tr. by Pierre Leyris and then in book form, with the acknowledgement 'traduit par l'auteur', Éditions de Minuit, 1960; *L'ultimo nastro di Krapp* (in *Teatro*).

FRAGMENT DE THÉÂTRE I, in 'Minuit', n. 8, mars 1974; *Theatre I*, Grove Press, New York 1976; *Teatro I*, in Samuel Beckett, *Racconti e teatro*, Einaudi, Torino 1978, tr. by Carlo Fruttero e Franco Lucentini [hereafter *Racconti e teatro*].

FRAGMENT DE THÉÂTRE II, in T. Bishop & R. Federman (eds.), *Samuel Beckett*, Éditions de l'Herne, Paris 1976; *Theatre II*, Grove Press, New York 1976; *Teatro II* (in *Racconti e teatro*).

EMBERS, in 'Evergreen Review', vol. 3, n. 10, Nov./December 1959; *Cendres*, in 'Les Lettres Nouvelles', n. 36, 30 décembre 1959, tr. by Robert Pinget and by Beckett; *Ceneri* (in *Teatro*).

HAPPY DAYS, Grove Press, New York 1961; *Oh les beaux jours*, Éditions de Minuit, Paris 1963; *Giorni felici* (in *Teatro*).

WORDS AND MUSIC, in 'Evergreen Review', vol. 6, n. 27, Nov./December 1962; *Paroles et Musique*, in *Comédies et actes divers*, Éditions de Minuit, Paris 1966; *Parole e Musica*, in Samuel Beckett, *Teatro*, Einaudi, Torino 1968, tr. by Carlo Fruttero [hereafter Teatro 1968].

ESQUISSE RADIOPHONIQUE, in 'Minuit', n. 5, septembre 1973; *Sketch for Radio Play*, in 'Stereo Headphones', n. 7, Spring 1976 and then with the title *Radio II* in *Ends and Odds*, Faber, London 1977; *Radio I* (in *Racconti e teatro*).

POCHADE RADIOPHONIQUE, in 'Minuit', n. 16, novembre 1975; *Radio II*, Grove Press, New York 1976; *Radio II* (in *Racconti e teatro*).

CASCANDO, *Dramatische Dichtungen*, Suhrkamp, Frankfurt 1963; *Cascando*, in *Comédie et actes divers* cit.; *Cascando* (in *Teatro* 1968).

PLAY, Faber, London 1964; *Comédie*, in 'Les Lettres Nouvelles', juin 1964; *Commedia* (in *Teatro* 1968).

FILM, Faber, London 1967; *Film*, in *Comédie et actes divers*, Éditions de Minuit, Paris 1972; *Film*, Einaudi, Torino 1985 (tr. by Maria Giovanna Andreolli).

COME AND GO, Calder and Boyars, London 1967; *Va-et-vient* in *Comédie et actes divers* cit.; Va e vieni (in *Teatro* 1968).

EH JOE, Faber, London 1967; *Dis Joe*, in *Comédie et actes divers* cit.; *Di' Joe* (in *Teatro* 1968).

BREATH, in 'Gambit', vol. 4, n. 16, 1970; *Souffle*, in 'Cahiers du chemin', n. 12, avril 1971; *Respiro* (in *Racconti e teatro*).

NOT I, Faber, London 1973; *Pas moi*, in 'Minuit', n. 12, janvier 1975; *Non io*, Einaudi, Torino 1974, tr. by John F. Lane).

THAT TIME, Faber, London 1976; *Cette fois*, in *Catastrophe et autres dramaticules*, Éditions de Minuit, Paris 1982; *Quella volta* (in *Racconti e teatro*).

FOOTFALLS, Faber, London 1976; *Pas*, in 'La Nouvelle Revue Française', n. 296, septembre 1977; *Passi* (in *Racconti e teatro*).

GHOST TRIO, Grove Press, New York 1976; *Trio degli spiriti* (in *Racconti e teatro*).

. . . BUT THE CLOUDS . . ., in *Ends and Odds*, Faber, London 1977; *. . . ma le nuvole . . .* (in *Racconti e teatro*).

A PIECE OF MONOLOGUE, 'Kenyon Review', New Series, I, iii, Summer 1979; *Solo*, in *Catastrophe et autres dramaticules* cit.; *Un pezzo di monologo*, in Samuel Beckett, *Tre pezzi d'occasione*, Einaudi, Torino 1982 (tr. by C. Fruttero e F. Lucentini).

ROCKABY, Grove Press, New York 1981; *Berceuse*, in *Catastrophe et autres dramaticules* cit.; *Dondolo* (in *Tre pezzi d'occasione*).

OHIO IMPROMPTU, in *Rockaby and Other Short Pieces*, Grove Press, New York 1981; *Impromptu d'Ohio*, in *Catastrophe et autres dramaticules*; *Dondolo* (in *Tre pezzi d'occasione*).

QUAD, in *Collected Shorter Plays*, Faber, London 1984; *Quad*, in Samuel Beckett, *Film*, Einaudi, Torino 1985, tr. by Camillo Pennati.

CATASTROPHE, Éditions de Minuit, Paris 1982; *Catastrophe*, 'New Yorker', 10 January 1983; *Catastrofe* (in *Film*).

NACHT UND TRÄUME, in *Collected Shorter Plays*; *Nacht und Träume* (in *Film*).

QUOI, in *Catastrophe et autres dramaticules*, Éditions de Minuit, Paris 1986; *What Where*, in *Collected Shorter Plays*; *Cosa dove* (in *Film*).

Critical Studies

A. Alvarez, *Beckett*, Fontana/Collins, London 1973.

C. Andonian, *Samuel Beckett: a Reference Guide*, G. K. Hall, Boston 1989.

L. Ben-Zvi, *Samuel Beckett*, Twayne, Boston 1986.

G. C. Bernard, *Samuel Beckett: a New Approach. A Study of the Novels and Plays*, Dent, London 1970.

P. Bertinetti, *Invito alla lettura di Beckett*, Mursia, Milano 1984.

E. Brater, *Beyond Minimalism. Beckett's Late Style in the Theater*, Oxford University Press, New York and Oxford 1987.

M. Bryden, *Women in Samuel Beckett's Prose and Drama*, Macmillan, London 1993 & Barnes and Noble, New York 1993.

L. St. J. Butler e R. J. Davis, *Rethinking Beckett*, Macmillan, London 1990.

J. Calder (ed), *As No Other Dare Fail. For Samuel Beckett on His 80th Birthday*, John Calder, London 1986.

P. Chabert (ed), *Samuel Beckett*, 'Revue d'Esthétique', numéro hors-sèrie, Éditions Jean-Michel Place, Paris 1990.

R. Cohn, *Samuel Beckett. The Comic Gamut*, Rutgers University Press, New Brunswick 1962.

R. Cohn, *Back to Beckett*, Princeton University Press, Princeton 1973.

R. Cohn, *Just Play: Beckett's Theater*, Princeton University Press, Princeton 1980.

S. Connor, *Samuel Beckett. Repetition, Theory and Text*, Basil Blackwell, Oxford/New York 1988.

V. Cooke, *Beckett on File*, Methuen, London 1985.

R. J. Davis e L. St. J. Butler, *Make Sense Who May. Essays on Samuel Beckett's Later Works*, C. Smythe, Gerrards Cross 1988 & Barnes and Nobles, Totowa (N. J.) 1988.

C. Duckworth (ed), Samuel Beckett, *En attendant Godot*, Harrap, London 1966.

G. Durozoi, *Beckett*, Bordas, Paris/Montréal 1972.

M. Esslin (ed), *Samuel Beckett. A Collection of Critical Essays*, Prentice-Hall, Englewood Cliffs (N. J.) 1965.

B. S. Fletcher e J. Fletcher, *A Student's Guide to the Plays of Samuel Beckett*, Faber and Faber, London 1978 e 1985.

J. Fletcher and J. Spurling, *Beckett. A Study of His Plays*, Eyre Methuen, London 1972.

M. Foucré, *Le geste et la parole dans le théâtre de Samuel Beckett*, Nizet, Paris 1970.

S. E. Gontarski, *The Intent of 'Undoing' in Samuel Beckett's Dramatic Texts*, Indiana University Press, Bloomington 1985.

L. Graver, *Waiting for Godot*, Landmarks of World Literature Series, Cambridge University Press, Cambridge 1989.

C. Hart, *Language and Structure in Beckett's Plays*, Colin Smythe, Gerrards Cross 1986.

S. Homan, *Beckett's Theaters: Interpretation for Performance*, Bucknell University Press, Lewisburg 1984.

L. Janvier, *Pour Samuel Beckett*, Éditions de Minuit, Paris 1966.

H. Kenner, *Samuel Beckett. A Critical Study*, Grove Press, New York 1961.

H. Kenner, *A Reader's Guide to Samuel Beckett*, Thames and Hudson, London 1973.

J. Knowlson, *Light and Darkness in the Theatre of Samuel Beckett*, Turret Books, London 1972.

J. Knowlson and J. Pilling, *Frescoes of the Skull. The Later Prose and Drama of Samuel Beckett*, Calder, London 1979.

C. Locatelli, *Unwording the World*, University of Pennsylvania Press, Philadelphia 1990.

C. R. Lyons, *Samuel Beckett*, Macmillan, London 1983.

D. McMillan e M. Fehsenfeld, *Beckett in the Theatre*, John Calder, London 1988 & Riverrun Press, New York 1988.

A. McMullan, *Theatre on Trial. Samuel Beckett's Later Drama*, Routledge, London 1993.

V. Mercier, *Beckett/Beckett*, Oxford University Press, New York 1977.

R. Oliva, *Beckett. Prima del silenzio*, Mursia, Milano 1967.

L. Perche, *Beckett, l'enfer à notre portée*, Éditions du Centurion, Paris 1969.

J. Pilling, *Samuel Beckett*, Henley, London 1976 & Routledge and Kegan Paul, Boston 1976.

R. Pountney, *Theatre of Shadows: Samuel Beckett's Drama 1956-1976*, Colin Smythe, Gerrards Cross e Barnes & Noble, Totowa (N. J.) 1988.

A. Simon, *Samuel Beckett*, Belfond, Paris 1983.

A. Tagliaferri, *Beckett e l'iperdeterminazione letteraria*, Feltrinelli, Milano 1967.

E. Webb, *The Plays of Samuel Beckett*, Peter Owen, London 1972.

K. Worth (ed), *Beckett the Shape-Changer*, Routledge and Kegan Paul, London 1976.

Biography

D. Bair, *Samuel Beckett: A Biography*, Harcourt Brace Jovanovich, New York 1978.

J. Knowlson, *Damned to Fame. The Life of Samuel Beckett*, Bloomsbury, London 1996.

Samuel Beckett circa 1930.

Jean Martin as Lucky and Roger Blin as Pozzo, 1953.

*Production by Samuel Beckett at the Schiller Theater,
Berlin in 1975.*

*Roman Polanski and Rufus in a production by
D. Asmus co-directed by Beckett.*

Rufus in a production by O. Krejca
at the Avignon Festival in 1979.

Production at the National Theatre, 1987.

CHRONOLOGY

Almost all the 'events' occurred in the first half of Beckett's life. From the end of the war, from when he immersed himself in the literary work which would make him one of the major figures in European culture in the second half of the twentieth century, the biography of Beckett virtually coincides with the dates of writing and production or publication of his works.

1906	Samuel Beckett is born in Dublin on 13 April, Good Friday, the second son of William Beckett and Mary Roe, both from well-to-do protestant families.
	Samuel and his older brother Frank spend a happy childhood in the Beckett's beautiful house in Foxrock, a residential suburb of Dublin.
1913	Is enrolled in Earlsfort House, a protestant school in Dublin.
1916	Easter Rising: William Beckett takes his sons to the top of a small hill from which they can see the fires blazing in the city of Dublin, marking the revolt against the English.
1920	Is sent to Portora Royal School at Enniskillen, in Ulster. It is a fairly strict school, which boasts Oscar Wilde among its ex-pupils.
1921	Becomes a member of the school's Literary and Scientific Society. Obtains brilliant results in his French studies.
1922	Is nominated Junior Prefect because of his athletic ability. Distinguishes himself in many sports: cricket, boxing, swimming and rugby.

1923   Enrols at Trinity College, Dublin, the most prestigious Irish University. Studies Italian and French. Becomes part of the entourage of Thomas Rudmose-Brown, Professor of French at Trinity, a distinguished expert not only in the classics but also in contemporary writing. Regularly attends the Dublin theatres; but is also very keen on silent films, an admirer of Chaplin and Keaton, Harold Lloyd, Ben Turpin, Laurel and Hardy and, later, the Marx Brothers.

1925   Becomes University golf champion.

1926   A brief stay in Tours. Does a bicycle tour of the Loire chateaux. On returning to Trinity meets Alfred Péron, a lecturer in French educated at the Ecole Normale Supérieure.

1927   Studies Déscartes, Baudelaire, Rimbaud and Apollinaire in depth; also Dante. During the summer visits Florence. In December completes his Bachelor of Arts, receiving a gold medal for his outstanding performance.

1928   During the summer goes to Kassel, in Germany, staying with his aunt, Cissy Sinclair, and meeting again his cousin Peggy, whom he had first met the previous year in Dublin and with whom he had fallen in love. However, Beckett breaks off their 'unofficial engagement'.

In October takes up an appointment as lecturer in English at the Ecole Normale in Paris. Meets Tom McGreevy , who had previously been a lecturer in English for two years. McGreevy introduces him to Joyce with whom the young Beckett establishes a close relationship, based on respect and admiration. Their Sunday walks in the Allée des Cygnes, on the Seine, have become part of the Beckett legend, as has Lucia Joyce's unreciprocated love for Beckett.

1929   Writes the essay *Dante . . . Bruno. Vico . . Joyce*, which will open the collection of articles intended to promote Joyce's *Work in Progress* (which will later become *Finnegans Wake*). During tennis matches with Alfred Péron meets Suzanne Deschevaux-Dusmenil, who nine years later will become his partner and whom he will marry 'secretly' at Folkstone in 1961.

1930   Together with Alfred Péron attempts the translation of the Anna Livia Plurabelle passage, the most famous section of *Work in Progress*. Writes the poem *Whoroscope*, with which he wins the poetry competition (and a small prize in money) organised by the Paris publishers, Hours Press. Writes an essay on Proust, which will be published the following year. Translates verse and prose of Eugenio Montale and Giovanni Comisso for the review 'This Quarter'.
In September returns to Dublin, where he is appointed as assistant in French at Trinity College.

1931   12 February: at the Peacock Theatre in Dublin acts the role of Don Diego in *Le Kid*, a parody of Corneille's *Le Cid*, which he wrote with Georges Pelorson, a lecturer in French.
At the beginning of June a violent quarrel takes place between Beckett and his mother, who was shocked and angered on reading some of her son's manuscripts. For several months, with Beckett in residence at Trinity college, there is no meeting between them.
Goes on a summer tour of France with his brother: they travel from Rouen through the Macon country (later referred to in *Godot*), the wines of which he appreciates, as far as the Cotes d'Azur, where he waits for Tom McGreevy. During the Christmas holidays visits Kassel, staying with his uncle and aunt. His cousin Peggy is already showing the first signs of the illness which within a few years will cause her death.

1932   From Germany, at the beginning of January sends his
            resignation to the academic authorities in Dublin. The
            decision is painful both because he knows Rudmose-
            Brown will be disappointed and above all because his
            father, so proud of his brilliant academic debut, will be
            very upset. But it is a decision which appears necessary to
            him (teaching seemed a grotesque job to him and above all
            represented an obstacle to his vocation as a writer).
            At the end of January leaves for Paris, where he takes a room
            at the Trianon Palace Hotel. Writes the novel *Dream of Fair to
            Middling Women*, which will remain unpublished until 1993.
            Often meets Joyce, resuming the ritual of the Sunday
            walks in the Allée des Cygnes. During the summer moves
            to London where he busies himself with the unlikely
            publication of the *Dream*. At the end of August returns to
            Ireland.
            The brilliant short story *Dante and the Lobster* is published
            in the December number of 'This Quarter'.

1933   Writes several short stories which will make up the
            collection *More Pricks Than Kicks*, the work by Beckett in
            which appear the most numerous and obvious
            autobiographical references.
            On 3 May has a neck operation. During his convalescence
            he learns that Peggy Sinclair died of tuberculosis on the
            day of his operation.
            On 28 June his father dies of a stroke. His father's death is
            a devastating loss to him.
            Towards the end of the year decides to move to London,
            where he will live on the small income (£200 a year) left
            him by his father.

1934   Lives in Gertrude Street, Chelsea. It is a very difficult
            period, marked by deep depression.
            A visit to Bethlem Royal Hospital in Beckenham gives him

the idea for the story and character of his first novel, *Murphy*, but after a short time he finds himself completely 'blocked', unable to work on the novel.

The collection of stories *More Pricks Than Kicks* is published by Chatto and Windus.

1935   Continues to work on *Murphy*; but his psychological state creates continual problems. He consults Dr W.R. Bion (of the Tavistock Clinic), who becomes his analyst.

In September attends a lecture by Jung at the Tavistock Clinic.

At the end of December, giving way to his mother's demands, he moves to Dublin.

1936   Falls in love with a rich young American, Betty Stockton. Finishes *Murphy* at the end of spring.

Towards the end of the year travels frequently in Germany, mainly visiting art galleries.

1937   In spring returns to Dublin, where his relationship with his mother becomes more and more strained.

In October moves to Paris, where he decides to settle permanently.

Works on a theatrical piece, *Human Wishes*, which will not be completed. Meets the van Velde brothers, Giacometti and Duchamp. Writes some poems in French, which will not be published until after the war.

In December Routledge accepts *Murphy* for publication, apparently after its rejection by forty-two other publishers.

1938   On 7 January is stabbed on the street by a stranger (when asked why, the assailant answers: 'I don't know, Monsieur'). In hospital receives a visit by Suzanne Deschevaux-Dumesnil, who had read in the newspaper the story of the attack on her old tennis partner. It is the beginning of a relationship which will last for life.

On 7 March *Murphy* appears in the London bookshops. Joyce offers his compliments and Dylan Thomas reviews the novel quite favourably.

In April moves to an apartment at 6, Rue des Favorites, where he will live until 1960.

1939	When Germany invades Poland in September, is on a visit to his mother in Dublin. Ireland is neutral, but Beckett decides to return to Paris ('Better France at war than Ireland in peace') and meets Suzanne and her anti-Nazi friends.
1940	On the invitation of Alfred Péron joins a resistance group 'Gloria', which is linked to the British Counter-Espionage in London (but not to De Gaulle). The group provides information to the allies on the movements of Nazi troops; Beckett works for the group as a translator and micro-photographer.
1941	On 13 January James Joyce dies in Zurich. A short time after Beckett meets by chance Joyce's secretary, Paul-Léopold Léon, who is Jewish. He tells him to flee immediately. 'I'll wait till tomorrow,' Léon answers, 'because my son has his final school examinations.' The next day Léon is arrested and the following year murdered.
1942	In August 'Gloria' is denounced . Alfred Péron is arrested and deported to a concentration camp (he will die in 1945, just after the arrival of the Americans). Suzanne and Beckett escape arrest by the Gestapo. They hide in Paris for a short time, the first night with Marcel Duchamp, then with some communist friends of Suzanne. They escape to the free zone, in the south of France. Towards the end of the year they settle in Roussillon, in the Vaucluse.

1943	A period of deepest depression for Beckett: he writes *Watt*, he says, to avoid going mad. But he also works as a farm-hand and takes part in the activities of Resistance groups.
1945	Leaves Roussillon in April. Goes to Dublin to see his mother. To enable him to re-enter France more quickly (his being an Irish citizen created bureaucratic problems) he offers himself as a volunteer at the Irish-run Red Cross hospital in Saint-Lô, a small town in Normandy destroyed by bombing. Works there as an interpreter and storekeeper from August to October. From Saint-Lô returns to Paris. Decides to make French his literary language.
1946	Writes the novel *Mercier et Camier* and the long narrative *Premier Amour*, both of which will be published in 1970. Writes the stories *L'expulsé*, published in the review 'Fontaine', and *Suite* , published in 'Temps Modernes'.
1947	Writes *Molloy,* the first novel of the Trilogy, and the play *Eleuthéria,* both in French.
1948	Writes *Malone meurt (Malone Dies),* the second novel of the *Trilogy.* Begins to write *Godot* in October.
1949	Finishes *Godot* in January. Starts work on the painful writing of *L'innomable* (The Unnamable), the third novel of the *Trilogy.*
1950	Finishes *L'innomable.* Writes the thirteen *Textes pour rien (Texts for Nothing).* Tristan Tzara reads *Godot* and expresses a very favourable opinion of it. On 25 August Beckett's mother dies. In November Jérome Lindon signs the contract for the publication of the *Trilogy* in the Éditions de Minuit.
1951	Publication by Minuit of *Molloy* and *Malone meurt.*

1952	Publication by Minuit of *En attendant Godot*.
1953	5 January: première of *En attendant Godot* at the Théatre de Babylone. Publication of *L'innomable* and *Watt*. Beckett translates *Godot* into English.
1954	22 November: première of the Italian version of *Waiting for Godot (Aspettando Godot)* at the Teatro di Via Vittoria di Roma, presented by Vittorio Caprioli's theatre company.
1955	Beckett struggles with the text of *Fin de partie (Endgame)* and begins to write, in English, a novel which he will never complete: *From an Abandoned Work*. English première of *Godot* at the Arts Theatre Club of London. Publication of *Nouvelles et Textes pour rien*.
1956	3 January: American première of *Godot*, in Miami. Finishes *Fin de partie*. Between July and September writes the radio play *All That Fall*.
1957	On 13 January the BBC broadcasts *All That Fall*. In February *Fin de partie* is published by Éditions de Minuit and on 3 April is produced in London (in French) at the Royal Court Theatre. The play is then transferred to the Studio des Champs-Elisées in Paris from the end of April.
1958	In the summer 'Evergreen Review' publishes *Krapp's Last Tape*, which has its first production in London, at the Royal Court Theatre, on 28 October.
1959	On 24 June the BBC broadcasts *Embers*, a radio play which wins the Premio Italia. Trinity College, Dublin, confers on Beckett the honorary degree of D. Litt. Beckett begins to write, in French, the work which will become *Comment c'est (How It Is)*.

1960   Publication of *Krapp* in French, under the title *La dernière bande,* which is produced in March at the Théatre Récamier in Paris (in January the American première had taken place at the Provincetown Playhouse in New York).

Beckett moves to the flat he has bought in Boulevard Saint-Jacques.

1961   The first months of the year are mainly occupied by the writing of *Happy Days*, on which he had begun work during the previous October.

Publication of *Comment c'est*.

17 September: world première of *Happy Days* at Cherry Lane Theatre in New York. Published by Grove Press.

Beckett, together with Borges, receives the Publishers' International Prize.

Writes the radio play *Words and Music.*

1962   Translates *Happy Days* into French, with the title *Oh, les beaux jours.*

1963   Writes *Play*, the world première of which takes place in Germany on 14 June, at the Ulmer Theatre in Ulm-Donau, in the German version, *Spiel*, by Erika and Elmar Tophoven. Publication of *Oh, les beaux jours.* The play is produced at the Twenty-second International Festival of the Teatro di Prosa at the Venice Biennial.

1964   Publication of *Play*, which is produced at the Cherry Lane Theatre in New York on 4 January and at the Old Vic in London on 7 April.

Goes to New York in July for the showing of the film (entitled simply *Film*), directed by Alan Schneider and starring Buster Keaton, which he wrote the previous year.

1965   During April Beckett begins to work on his first television play, *Eh Joe. Film* is shown at the Venice Film Festival, where it is very favourably received by the more perceptive critics.

1966	4 July: BBC broadcast of *Eh Joe*.
1967	25 September: *Endgame*, directed by Beckett himself, produced at the Schiller Theatre in Berlin.
1968	His aunt Peggy, for whom he felt great affection, dies in March. Beckett goes to Ireland for the funeral. He is struck by a very serious lung infection, which from May forces him to remain at home for many weeks. Only in September is there a definite improvement in his condition, but his convalescence is very long. At the beginning of December Beckett and his wife leave for the island of Madeira; from there they move, in the middle of December, to the island of Porto Santo, where they stay for about three months.
1969	In June Kenneth Tynan produces his 'scandalous' *Oh! Calcutta* in New York, opening with *Breath*, a very short work sent him by Beckett. Beckett is awarded the Nobel Prize for Literature. The prize is accepted at Stockholm by his publisher Jérome Lindon, while Beckett is in Tunisia.
1970	In October has a cataract operation.
1971	In February undergoes a second eye operation; but his sight rapidly improves. From June is in Santa Margherita Ligure, where he works on his production of *Happy Days* for the Schiller Theatre. At the beginning of August is in Berlin for the beginning of rehearsals.
1972	22 November: world première of *Not I* at Lincoln Center in New York.
1973	16 January: *Not I* produced at the Royal Court in London: the actress is Billie Whitelaw. The work published by Faber.
1975	Beckett's production of *Godot* presented at the Schiller Theatre in Berlin.

Directs *Pas moi*, the French version of *Not I*, with Madeleine Renaud as interpreter: the première is on 8 April, at the Théatre d'Orsay.

In August completes *That Time,* on which he has been working since the previous year. Writes *Footfalls*.

1976   Writes the television piece *Ghost Trio*.

In May the triple bill *That Time*, *Footfalls* and *Play* are produced at the Royal Court in London: it is a seventieth birthday present to Beckett.

In October – November writes . . . *but the clouds* . . ., a work for television.

1977   17 April: the BBC broadcasts *Ghost Trio* and . . . *but the clouds* . . . .

1978   Minuit publishes the French translation of *Footfalls*, under the title *Pas*.

In April Beckett directs *Pas* (with Delphine Seyrig and Madeleine Renaud) at the Théatre d'Orsay. Also directs the Berlin production of *Spiel*.

1979   At the Royal Court, London, directs Billie Whitelaw in a remarkable production of *Happy Days*.

The 'Kenyon Review' publishes *A Piece of Monologue*, which David Warrilow interprets at the La Mama Theatre in New York in December.

1980   The short story *Company* and its French translation, *Compagnie,* is published by Calder and Minuit respectively.

1981   Minuit publishes *Mal vu mal dit*; Grove Press publishes the English version, *Ill Seen Ill Said*.

Ohio State University organises a conference dedicated to Beckett, during which (9 May) David Warrilow acts *Ohio Impromptu*, a sketch written by Beckett for the occasion.

Beckett writes *Quad*, a work for television, which is broadcast by German television on 8 October.

1982   Writes *Catastrophe*, dedicated to the writer Vaclav Havel, who was being persecuted at that time by the Czechoslovakian regime. The work is produced at the Avignon Festival.

Writes *Nacht und Traume*, a work for Television which German television will transmit the following year.

1983   'The New Yorker' publishes in its number for 10 January the English version of *Catastrophe*, which is presented at the Harold Clurman Theatre in New York in June.

Beckett writes *Quoi où* in French and immediately translates it into English, with the title *What Where*, for the performance at the Harold Clurman Theatre.

1985   Adapts *Quoi où* for German television.

1986   Pierre Chabert produces *Quoi où* at the Rond-Point in Paris, in the version revised by Beckett in the light of the television production.

1988   Kept in hospital for more than a month and following that is forced to spend some time in a rest home not far from his own home.

Writes a brief prose work called *Stirrings Still.*

1989   Translates *Stirrings Still* into French, with the title *Soubresauts.*

17 July: Beckett's wife, Suzanne, dies and is buried in the cemetery of Montparnasse.

Minuit publishes *Soubresauts* in October.

Beckett enters hospital at the beginning of December. Dies on 22 December. His funeral, a very private affair, takes place on 26 December, at the cemetery of Montparnasse.

PHONETIC SYMBOLS

Vowels

[ɪ]	*as in*	six
[i]	"	happy
[iː]	"	see
[e]	"	red
[æ]	"	hat
[ɑː]	"	car
[ɒ]	"	dog
[ɔː]	"	door
[ʊ]	"	put
[uː]	"	food
[ʌ]	"	cup
[ə]	"	about
[ɜː]	"	girl

Diphthongs

[eɪ]	*as in*	made
[aɪ]	"	five
[aʊ]	"	house
[ɔɪ]	"	boy
[əʊ]	"	home
[ɪə]	"	beer
[eə]	"	hair
[ʊə]	"	poor

Consonants

[b]	*as in*	bed
[k]	"	cat
[tʃ]	"	church
[d]	"	day
[f]	"	foot
[g]	"	good
[dʒ]	"	page
[h]	"	how
[j]	"	yes
[l]	"	leg
[m]	"	mum
[n]	"	nine
[ŋ]	"	sing
[p]	"	pen
[r]	"	red
[s]	"	soon
[z]	"	zoo
[ʃ]	"	show
[ʒ]	"	measure
[t]	"	tea
[θ]	"	thin
[ð]	"	this
[v]	"	voice
[w]	"	wine

[']   represents primary stress in the syllable which follows

[ˌ]   represents secondary stress in the syllable which follows

[ʳ]   indicates that the final 'r' is only pronounced before a word beginning with a vowel sound (British English). In American English, the 'r' is usually pronounced before both consonants and vowel sounds.

Manuscript of Waiting for Godot.

Waiting for Godot

A C T I V I T I E S

Pre-reading Questions

1. Beckett's work is often interpreted in terms of its relation to modernism and post-modernism. Find out what you can about these.

2. Check the meaning of the word 'absurd' in a good dictionary.

3. Find out what you can about 'the Theatre of the Absurd'.

4. Beckett subtitled the work: *A Tragicomedy in Two Acts*. What do you understand by 'tragicomedy'?

5. Try to see a Laurel and Hardy film. Note their comic routines and the way they are dressed. (If possible it would also be useful to see some silent films with Charlie Chaplin and Buster Keaton.)

6. What does the word 'Godot' in the title suggest to you?

Act I

The Characters

ESTRAGON

VLADIMIR

LUCKY

POZZO

A BOY

These symbols indicate the beginning and end of the passages recorded on the accompanying CD.

A country road. A tree. Evening

Estragon, Sitting on a low mound, [1] *is trying to take off his boot. He pulls at it with both hands, panting. He gives up, exhausted, rests, tries again. As before.*
Enter Vladimir.

ESTRAGON *(giving up again).* Nothing to be done. [2]

VLADIMIR *(advancing with short, stiff strides, legs wide apart).* [3] I'm beginning to come round to that opinion. All my life I've tried to put it from me, saying, Vladimir, be reasonable, you haven't yet tried everything. And I resumed the struggle. *(He broods, musing on the struggle. Turning to Estragon.)* So there you are again.

ESTRAGON. Am I?

VLADIMIR. I'm glad to see you back. I thought you were gone for ever.

ESTRAGON. Me too.

1. *mound* [maʊnd] : elevation of earth or stones, especially of earth heaped on a grave.
2. *Nothing to be done* : the phrase becomes a kind of refrain in the play, suggesting Vladimir and Estragon's sense of hopelessness.
3. *legs wide apart* : Vladimir suffers from enlargement of the prostate gland, a painful and quite common complaint in old men, which accounts for the stiffness of his walk and for his frequent desire to pass water.

VLADIMIR. Together again at last! We'll have to celebrate this. But how? *(He reflects.)* Get up till I embrace you. [1]

ESTRAGON *(irritably)*. Not now, not now.

VLADIMIR *(hurt, coldly)*. May one enquire where His Highness [2] spent the night?

ESTRAGON. In a ditch. Fosso

VLADIMIR *(admiringly)*. A ditch! Where?

ESTRAGON *(without gesture)*. Over there.

VLADIMIR. And they didn't beat you?

ESTRAGON. Beat me? Certainly they beat me.

VLADIMIR. The same lot as usual?

ESTRAGON. The same? I don't know.

VLADIMIR. When I think of it... all these years... but for me... where would you be...? *(Decisively.)* You'd be nothing more than a little heap of bones at the present minute, no doubt about it.

ESTRAGON. And what of it?

VLADIMIR *(gloomily)*. It's too much for one man. *(Pause. Cheerfully.)* On the other hand what's the good of losing heart now, that's what I say. We should have thought of it a million years ago, in the nineties.

ESTRAGON. Ah stop blathering [3] and help me off with this bloody thing.

VLADIMIR. Hand in hand from the top of the Eiffel Tower, [4]

1. *Get up till I embrace you* : this use of 'till' is Irish.
2. *His Highness* : Vladimir addresses Estragon as if he were royalty.
3. *blathering* : talking nonsense.
4. *Hand in hand from the top of the Eiffel Tower* : Vladimir is regretting that they didn't commit suicide by jumping together from the top of the Eiffel Tower, while they still looked respectable enough to be admitted to the tower.

among the first. We were presentable in those days. Now it's too late. They wouldn't even let us up. *(Estragon tears at his boot.)* What are you doing?

ESTRAGON. Taking off my boot. Did that never happen to you?

VLADIMIR. Boots must be taken off every day, I'm tired telling you that. Why don't you listen to me?

ESTRAGON *(feebly)*. Help me!

VLADIMIR. It hurts?

ESTRAGON. Hurts! He wants to know if it hurts!

VLADIMIR *(angrily)*. No one ever suffers but you. I don't count. I'd like to hear what you'd say if you had what I have.

ESTRAGON. It hurts?

VLADIMIR. Hurts! He wants to know if it hurts!

ESTRAGON *(pointing)*. You might button it all the same.

VLADIMIR *(stooping)*. True. *(He buttons his fly.)* [1] Never neglect the little things of life. [2]

ESTRAGON. What do you expect, you always wait till the last moment. [3]

VLADIMIR *(musingly)*. The last moment… *(He meditates.)* Hope deferred maketh the something sick, [4] who said that?

ESTRAGON. Why don't you help me?

---

1. *fly* : zipped or buttoned opening down the front of the trousers.
2. *the little things of life* : a) the buttons Vladimir had not done up; b) his penis.
3. *the last moment* : a) Vladimir always waits to the last moment to urinate; b) the Day of Judgement.
4. *Hope deferred maketh the something sick* : Proverbs 13:12: 'Hope deferred maketh the heart sick.' Beckett often quotes from the Bible and Shakespeare. Note the archaic form 'maketh' for 'makes'. The quotation continues: '…but when the desire cometh, it is a tree of life.'

VLADIMIR. Sometimes I feel it coming all the same. Then I go all queer. [1] *(He takes off his hat, peers inside it, feels about inside it, shakes it, puts it on again.)* How shall I say? Relieved and at the same time... *(he searches for the word)...* appalled. [2] *(With emphasis.)* AP-PALLED. *(He takes off his hat again, peers inside it.)* Funny. *(He knocks on the crown as though to dislodge a foreign body, peers into it again, puts it on again.)* Nothing to be done. *(Estragon with a supreme effort succeeds in pulling off his boot. He looks inside it, feels about inside it, turns it upside down, shakes it, looks on the ground to see if anything has fallen out, finds nothing, feels inside it again, staring sightlessly before him.)* Well?

ESTRAGON. Nothing.

VLADIMIR. Show.

ESTRAGON. There's nothing to show.

VLADIMIR. Try and put it on again.

ESTRAGON *(examining his foot)*. I'll air it for a bit.

VLADIMIR. There's man all over for you, [3] blaming on his boots the faults of his feet. *(He takes off his hat again, peers inside it, feels about inside it, knocks on the crown, blows into it, puts it on again.)* This is getting alarming. *(Silence. Vladimir deep in thought, Estragon pulling at his toes.)* One of the thieves was saved. *(Pause.)* It's a reasonable percentage. [4] *(Pause.)* Gogo.

---

1. *go all queer* : begin to feel strange.
2. *appalled* [ə'pɔːld] : dismayed (etymologically 'become pale').
3. *There's man all over for you* : that's a typical way for man to behave.
4. *One of the thieves was saved . . . It's a reasonable percentage* : This idea also occurs in Beckett's *Murphy*. The author said he had been struck by the symmetry of a sentence of St. Augustine: 'Do not despair – one of the thieves was saved; do not presume – one of the thieves was damned.' He also suggested the equal chance of 'salvation' and 'damnation' for Estragon's feet, since he has trouble with one of his two boots.

ESTRAGON. What?

VLADIMIR. Suppose we repented.

ESTRAGON. Repented what?

VLADIMIR. Oh… *(He reflects.)* We wouldn't have to go into the
    details.

ESTRAGON. Our being born? [1]

> *Vladimir breaks into a hearty laugh which he immediately
> stifles, his hand pressed to his pubis, his face contorted.*

VLADIMIR. One daren't even laugh any more.

ESTRAGON. Dreadful privation.

VLADIMIR. Merely smile. *(He smiles suddenly from ear to ear, keeps
    smiling, ceases as suddenly.)* It's not the same thing.
    Nothing to be done. *(Pause.)* Gogo.

ESTRAGON *(irritably)*. What is it?

VLADIMIR. Did you ever read the Bible?

ESTRAGON. The Bible… *(He reflects.)* I must have taken a look at it.

VLADIMIR. Do you remember the Gospels?

ESTRAGON. I remember the maps of the Holy Land. Coloured
    they were. Very pretty. The Dead Sea was pale blue.
    The very look of it made me thirsty. That's where
    we'll go, I used to say, that's where we'll go for our
    honeymoon. We'll swim. We'll be happy.

VLADIMIR. You should have been a poet.

ESTRAGON. I was. *(Gesture towards his rags.)* Isn't that obvious.

> *Silence.*

VLADIMIR. Where was I… How's your foot?

---

1. *Our being born?* : In his essay on Proust Beckett quotes Calderón:
    'Man's greatest sin is to have been born.' The same quotation
    can also be found in Schopenhauer, whose works Beckett had
    studied with great interest.

ESTRAGON. Swelling visibly.

VLADIMIR. Ah yes, the two thieves. Do you remember the story?

ESTRAGON. No.

VLADIMIR. Shall I tell it to you?

ESTRAGON. No.

VLADIMIR. It'll pass the time. *(Pause.)* Two thieves, crucified at the same time as our Saviour. One –

ESTRAGON. Our what?

VLADIMIR. Our Saviour. Two thieves. One is supposed to have been saved and the other... *(he searches for the contrary of saved)...* damned.

ESTRAGON. Saved from what?

VLADIMIR. Hell.

ESTRAGON. I'm going.

He does not move.

VLADIMIR. And yet... *(pause)...* how is it—this is not boring you I hope—how is it that of the four Evangelists only one speaks of a thief being saved. The four of them were there—or thereabout—and—only one speaks of a thief being saved. [1] *(Pause.)* Come on, Gogo, return the ball, can't you, once in a way?

ESTRAGON *(with exaggerated enthusiasm)*. I find this really most extraordinarily interesting.

VLADIMIR. One out of four. Of the other three two don't mention any thieves at all and the third says that both of them abused him. [2]

---

1. *...only one speaks of a thief being saved* : Luke 23:43: 'Verily I say unto thee, To day shalt thou be with me in paradise.' Neary, a character in *Murphy*, refers to the same idea: 'Do not despair... Remember also one thief was saved.'

2. *...the third says that both of them abused him* : Matthew 27:44: 'The thieves also, which were crucified with him, cast the same in his teeth.'

ESTRAGON. Who?

VLADIMIR. What?

ESTRAGON. What's all this about? Abused who?

VLADIMIR. The Saviour.

ESTRAGON. Why?

VLADIMIR. Because he wouldn't save them.

ESTRAGON. From hell?

VLADIMIR. Imbecile! From death.

ESTRAGON. I thought you said hell.

VLADIMIR. From death, from death.

ESTRAGON. Well what of it?

VLADIMIR. Then the two of them must have been damned.

ESTRAGON. And why not?

VLADIMIR. But one of the four says that one of the two was saved.

ESTRAGON. Well? They don't agree, and that's all there is to it.

VLADIMIR. But all four were there. And only one speaks of a thief
        being saved. Why believe him rather than the others?

ESTRAGON. Who believes him?

VLADIMIR. Everybody. It's the only version they know.

ESTRAGON. People are bloody ignorant apes. [1]

> *He rises painfully, goes limping to extreme left, halts, gazes
> into distance off with his hand screening his eyes, turns, goes
> to extreme right, gazes into distance. Vladimir watches him,
> then goes and picks up the boot, peers into it, drops it hastily.*

VLADIMIR. Pah!

> *He spits. Estragon moves to centre, halts with his back to
> auditorium.*

---

1. *apes* : tailless monkeys. The word is used to describe people who
   imitate without thinking.

ESTRAGON. Charming spot. *(He turns, advances to front, halts facing auditorium.)* Inspiring prospects.[1] *(He turns to Vladimir.)* Let's go.

VLADIMIR. We can't.

ESTRAGON. Why not?

VLADIMIR. We're waiting for Godot.[2]

ESTRAGON *(despairingly)*. Ah! *(Pause.)* You're sure it was here?

VLADIMIR. What?

ESTRAGON. That we were to wait.

VLADIMIR. He said by the tree. *(They look at the tree.)* Do you see any others?

ESTRAGON. What is it?

VLADIMIR. I don't know. A willow.

ESTRAGON. Where are the leaves?

VLADIMIR. It must be dead.

ESTRAGON. No more weeping.

VLADIMIR. Or perhaps it's not the season.

ESTRAGON. Looks to me more like a bush.[3]

VLADIMIR. A shrub.[4]

---

1. I*nspiring prospects* : Estragon's comment on the audience is one of those 'metatheatrical' moments referred to in the introduction.

2. *We're waiting for Godot* : Colin Duckworth (See his edition of *En attendant Godot*, Harrap, London, 1966, p. 1 – 1.i) tells us that in the manuscript Vladimir and Estragon have a written contract with Godot but, since a written agreement would make Godot's existence too definite, Beckett dropped the idea from the published version. Beckett told Roger Blin, his first producer, that the name Godot was suggested to him by *godillots* and godasses, French slang words for boots.

3. *bush* : a shrub or clump of shrubs with stems of moderate length. The two men are arguing about a small, almost non-existent, distinction.

4. *shrub* : a woody plant smaller than a tree.

ESTRAGON. A bush.

VLADIMIR. A—. What are you insinuating? That we've come to
the wrong place?

ESTRAGON. He should be here.

VLADIMIR. He didn't say for sure he'd come.

ESTRAGON. And if he doesn't come?

VLADIMIR. We'll come back tomorrow.

ESTRAGON. And then the day after tomorrow.

VLADIMIR. Possibly.

ESTRAGON. And so on.

VLADIMIR. The point is—

ESTRAGON. Until he comes.

VLADIMIR. You're merciless.

ESTRAGON. We came here yesterday.

VLADIMIR. Ah no, there you're mistaken.

ESTRAGON. What did we do yesterday?

VLADIMIR. What did we do yesterday?

ESTRAGON. Yes.

VLADIMIR. Why... (Angrily). Nothing is certain when you're
about.

ESTRAGON. In my opinion we were here.

VLADIMIR (looking round). You recognize the place?

ESTRAGON. I didn't say that.

VLADIMIR. Well?

ESTRAGON. That makes no difference.

VLADIMIR. All the same... that tree... (turning towards the
auditorium)... that bog. [1]

1. *that bog* : Estragon suggests the audience is sitting in a bog. Given
    all the other vulgarisms in *Godot*, there is probably a play on two
    senses of 'bog': a) wet, marshy ground; b) lavatory (slang).

ESTRAGON. You're sure it was this evening?

VLADIMIR. What?

ESTRAGON. That we were to wait.

VLADIMIR. He said Saturday. *(Pause.)* I think.

ESTRAGON. You think.

VLADIMIR. I must have made a note of it.

> *He fumbles in his pockets, bursting with miscellaneous rubbish.*

ESTRAGON *(very insidious)*. But what Saturday? And is it Saturday? Is it not rather Sunday? *(Pause.)* Or Monday? *(Pause.)* Or Friday?

VLADIMIR *(looking wildly about him, as though the date was inscribed in the landscape)*. It's not possible!

ESTRAGON. Or Thursday?

VLADIMIR. What'll we do?

ESTRAGON. If he came yesterday and we weren't here you may be sure he won't come again today.

VLADIMIR. But you say we were here yesterday.

ESTRAGON. I may be mistaken. *(Pause.)* Let's stop talking for a minute, do you mind?

VLADIMIR *(feebly)*. All right. *(Estragon sits down on the mound. Vladimir paces agitatedly to and fro, halting from time to time to gaze into distance off. Estragon falls asleep. Vladimir halts before Estragon.)* Gogo!... Gogo!... GOGO!

> *Estragon wakes with a start.*

ESTRAGON *(restored to the horror of his situation)*. I was asleep! *(Despairingly.)* Why will you never let me sleep?

VLADIMIR. I felt lonely.

ESTRAGON. I had a dream.

VLADIMIR. Don't tell me!

ESTRAGON. I dreamt that—

VLADIMIR. DON'T TELL ME!

ESTRAGON *(gesture towards the universe)*. This one is enough for you? [1] *(Silence.)* It's not nice of you, Didi. Who am I to tell my private nightmares to if I can't tell them to you?

VLADIMIR. Let them remain private. You know I can't bear that.

ESTRAGON *(coldly)*. There are times when I wonder if it wouldn't be better for us to part.

VLADIMIR. You wouldn't go far.

ESTRAGON. That would be too bad, really too bad. *(Pause.)* Wouldn't it, Didi, be really too bad? *(Pause.)* When you think of the beauty of the way. *(Pause.)* And the goodness of the wayfarers. [2] *(Pause. Wheedling.)* Wouldn't it, Didi?

VLADIMIR. Calm yourself.

ESTRAGON *(voluptuously)*. Calm... calm... The English say cawm. [3] *(Pause.)* You know the story of the Englishman in the brothel?

VLADIMIR. Yes.

ESTRAGON. Tell it to me.

VLADIMIR. Ah stop it!

1. *This one is enough for you?* : Estragon's dream was evidently a nightmare. He is asking Vladimir if the nightmare of the universe is already enough for him, without his having the story of Estragon's nightmare inflicted on him.

2. *... the beauty of the way ... And the goodness of the wayfarers* : Words that have a Biblical feel about them. Estragon is obviously being ironical.

3. *cawm* [kɔːm] : this pronunciation is a parody of an upper-class English accent.

ESTRAGON. An Englishman having drunk a little more than usual goes to a brothel. [1] The bawd [2] asks him if he wants a fair one, a dark one, or a red-haired one. Go on.

VLADIMIR. STOP IT!

> *Exit Vladimir hurriedly. Estragon gets up and follows him as far as the limit of the stage. Gestures of Estragon like those of a spectator encouraging a pugilist. Enter Vladimir. He brushes past Estragon, crosses the stage with bowed head. Estragon takes a step towards him, halts.*

ESTRAGON *(gently)*. You wanted to speak to me? *(Silence. Estragon takes a step forward.)* You had something to say to me? *(Silence. Another step forward.)* Didi…

VLADIMIR *(without turning)*. I've nothing to say to you.

ESTRAGON *(step forward)*. You're angry? *(Silence. Step forward.)* Forgive me. *(Silence. Step forward. Estragon lays his hand on Vladimir's shoulder.)* Come, Didi. *(Silence.)* Give me your hand. *(Vladimir half turns.)* Embrace me! *(Vladimir stiffens.)* Don't be stubborn! *(Vladimir softens. They embrace. Estragon recoils.)* You stink of garlic!

VLADIMIR. It's for the kidneys. *(Silence. Estragon looks attentively at the tree.)* What do we do now?

ESTRAGON. Wait.

VLADIMIR. Yes, but while waiting.

ESTRAGON. What about hanging ourselves?

VLADIMIR. Hmm. It'd give us an erection!

ESTRAGON *(highly excited)*. An erection!

1. *An Englishman having drunk a little more than usual goes to a brothel* : reference to an obscene French joke involving the alleged English preference for sodomy. Ruby Cohn gives it in full in *Journal of Beckett Studies* (Winter 1976), p. 42, note 2.
2. *bawd* : keeper of the brothel.

VLADIMIR. With all that follows. Where it falls mandrakes[1] grow. That's why they shriek when you pull them up. Did you not know that?

ESTRAGON. Let's hang ourselves immediately!

VLADIMIR. From a bough? *(They go towards the tree.)* I wouldn't trust it.

ESTRAGON. We can always try.

VLADIMIR. Go ahead.

ESTRAGON. After you.

VLADIMIR. No no, you first.

ESTRAGON. Why me?

VLADIMIR. You're lighter than I am.

ESTRAGON. Just so!

VLADIMIR. I don't understand.

ESTRAGON. Use your intelligence, can't you?

Vladimir uses his intelligence.

VLADIMIR *(finally).* I remain in the dark.

ESTRAGON. This is how it is. *(He reflects.)* The bough... the bough... *(Angrily).* Use your head, can't you?

VLADIMIR. You're my only hope.

ESTRAGON *(with effort).* Gogo light—bough not break—Gogo dead. Didi heavy—bough break—Didi alone. Whereas—

VLADIMIR. I hadn't thought of that.

---

1. *mandrakes* : The mandrake is a plant the forked root of which was said to be of human shape. Genesis 30 suggests that the fruit when eaten by women promotes conception. Vladimir refers to the ancient belief that mandrakes grew where human sperm fell. They grew beneath gibbets because it was believed they were fertilised by the sperm of hanged men, who ejaculated at the moment of hanging.

ESTRAGON. If it hangs you it'll hang anything.

VLADIMIR. But am I heavier than you?

ESTRAGON. So you tell me. I don't know. There's an even chance. Or nearly.

VLADIMIR. Well? What do we do?

ESTRAGON. Don't let's do anything. It's safer.

VLADIMIR. Let's wait and see what he says.

ESTRAGON. Who?

VLADIMIR. Godot.

ESTRAGON. Good idea.

VLADIMIR. Let's wait till we know exactly how we stand.

ESTRAGON. On the other hand it might be better to strike the iron before it freezes. [1]

VLADIMIR. I'm curious to hear what he has to offer. Then we'll take it or leave it.

ESTRAGON. What exactly did we ask him for?

VLADIMIR. Were you not there?

ESTRAGON. I can't have been listening.

VLADIMIR. Oh… nothing very definite.

ESTRAGON. A kind of prayer.

VLADIMIR. Precisely.

ESTRAGON. A vague supplication.

VLADIMIR. Exactly.

ESTRAGON. And what did he reply?

VLADIMIR. That he'd see.

ESTRAGON. That he couldn't promise anything.

---

1. *strike the iron before it freezes* : 'a characteristic Beckettian twist on a popular cliché' (Fletcher et al). The normal expression is: 'strike while the iron is hot' (act while conditions are favourable).

VLADIMIR. That he'd have to think it over.

ESTRAGON. In the quiet of his home.

VLADIMIR. Consult his family.

ESTRAGON. His friends.

VLADIMIR. His agents.

ESTRAGON. His correspondents.

VLADIMIR. His books.

ESTRAGON. His bank account.

VLADIMIR. Before taking a decision.

ESTRAGON. It's the normal thing.

VLADIMIR. Is it not?

ESTRAGON. I think it is.

VLADIMIR. I think so too.

   Silence.

ESTRAGON *(anxious)*. And we?

VLADIMIR. I beg your pardon?

ESTRAGON. I said, And we?

VLADIMIR. I don't understand.

ESTRAGON. Where do we come in?

VLADIMIR. Come in?

ESTRAGON. Take your time.

VLADIMIR. Come in? On our hands and knees. [1]

ESTRAGON. As bad as that?

---

1. *Come in? On our hands and knees* : Estragon asks 'Where do we come in?' in the sense of 'What is our role in this?' but Vladimir interprets the expression 'come in' literally, saying that they come in on their hands and knees, which is appropriate to their desperate situation.

VLADIMIR. Your Worship [1] wishes to assert his prerogatives?

ESTRAGON. We've no rights any more?

Laugh of Vladimir, stifled as before, less the smile.

VLADIMIR. You'd make me laugh, if it wasn't prohibited.

ESTRAGON. We've lost our rights?

VLADIMIR *(distinctly)*. We got rid of them.

Silence. They remain motionless, arms dangling, heads sunk, sagging at the knees.

ESTRAGON *(feebly)*. We're not tied? [2] *(Pause.)* We're not—

VLADIMIR. Listen!

They listen, grotesquely rigid.

ESTRAGON. I hear nothing.

VLADIMIR. Hssst! *(They listen. Estragon loses his balance, almost falls. He clutches the arm of Vladimir, who totters. They listen, huddled together.)* [3] Nor I.

Sighs of relief. They relax and separate.

ESTRAGON. You gave me a fright.

VLADIMIR. I thought it was he.

ESTRAGON. Who?

VLADIMIR. Godot.

ESTRAGON. Pah! The wind in the reeds. [4]

---

1. *Your Worship* : Vladimir again ironically addresses Estragon as an eminent person as he had on p. 6, when he called him Your Highness.
2. *tied* : a) legally bound; b) physically bound, as with a rope.
3. *Huddled* ['hʌdəld] *together* : crowded together, like sheep, for example.
4. *The wind in the reeds* : in Luke 7:24 Jesus alludes to John the Baptist as 'a reed shaken by the wind'. John came to herald one greater than he but was not recognised by the people.

VLADIMIR. I could have sworn I heard shouts.

ESTRAGON. And why would he shout?

VLADIMIR. At his horse.

Silence.

ESTRAGON *(violently)*. I'm hungry.

VLADIMIR. Do you want a carrot?

ESTRAGON. Is that all there is?

VLADIMIR. I might have some turnips.

ESTRAGON. Give me a carrot. *(Vladimir rummages* [1] *in his pockets, takes out a turnip and gives it to Estragon who takes a bite out of it. Angrily.)* It's a turnip!

VLADIMIR. Oh pardon! I could have sworn it was a carrot. *(He rummages again in his pockets, finds nothing but turnips.)* All that's turnips. *(He rummages.)* You must have eaten the last. *(He rummages.)* Wait, I have it. *(He brings out a carrot and gives it to Estragon.)* There, dear fellow. *(Estragon wipes the carrot on his sleeve and begins to eat it.)* Give me the turnip. *(Estragon gives back the turnip which Vladimir puts in his pocket.)* Make it last, that's the end of them.

ESTRAGON *(chewing)*. I asked you a question.

VLADIMIR. Ah.

ESTRAGON. Did you reply?

VLADIMIR. How's the carrot.

ESTRAGON. It's a carrot.

VLADIMIR. So much the better, so much the better. *(Pause.)* What was it you wanted to know?

ESTRAGON. I've forgotten. *(Chews.)* That's what annoys me. *(He looks at the carrot appreciatively, dangles it between finger*

---

1. *rummages* ['rʌmɪdʒəz] : searches thoroughly.

and thumb.) I'll never forget this carrot. *(He sucks the end of it meditatively.)* Ah yes, now I remember.

VLADIMIR. Well?

ESTRAGON *(his mouth full, vacuously)*. We're not tied!

VLADIMIR. I don't hear a word you're saying.

ESTRAGON *(chews, swallows)*. I'm asking you if we're tied.

VLADIMIR. Tied?

ESTRAGON. Ti-ed.

VLADIMIR. How do you mean tied?

ESTRAGON. Down.

VLADIMIR. But to whom. By whom?

ESTRAGON. To your man.

VLADIMIR. To Godot? Tied to Godot? What an idea! No question of it. *(Pause.)* For the moment.

ESTRAGON. His name is Godot?

VLADIMIR. I think so.

ESTRAGON. Fancy that. *(He raises what remains of the carrot by the stub of leaf, twirls it before his eyes.)* Funny, the more you eat the worse it gets.

VLADIMIR. With me it's just the opposite.

ESTRAGON. In other words?

VLADIMIR. I get used to the muck [1] as I go along.

ESTRAGON *(after prolonged reflection)*. Is that the opposite?

VLADIMIR. Question of temperament.

ESTRAGON. Of character.

VLADIMIR. Nothing you can do about it.

ESTRAGON. No use struggling.

VLADIMIR. One is what one is.

---

1. *muck* : rubbish.

ESTRAGON. No use wriggling.

VLADIMIR. The essential doesn't change.

ESTRAGON. Nothing to be done. *(He proffers the remains of the carrot to Vladimir.)* Like to finish it?

> *A terrible cry, close at hand. Estragon drops the carrot. They remain motionless, then together make a sudden rush towards the wings. Estragon stops half-way, runs back, picks up the carrot, stuffs it in his pocket, runs towards Vladimir who is waiting for him, stops again, runs back, picks up his boot, runs to rejoin Vladimir. Huddled together, shoulders hunched, [1] cringing away [2] from the menace, they wait.*
> *Enter Pozzo and Lucky. [3] Pozzo drives Lucky by means of a rope passed round his neck, so that Lucky is the first to appear, followed by the rope which is long enough to allow him to reach the middle of the stage before Pozzo appears. Lucky carries a heavy bag, a folding stool, [4] a picnic basket and a greatcoat. Pozzo a whip.*

POZZO *(off)*. On! *(Crack of whip. Pozzo appears. They cross the stage. Lucky passes before Vladimir and Estragon and exit. Pozzo at the sight of Vladimir and Estragon stops short. The rope tautens. [5] Pozzo jerks it violently.)* Back!

> *Noise of Lucky falling with all his baggage. Vladimir and Estragon turn towards him, half wishing half fearing to go to his assistance. Vladimir takes a step towards Lucky, Estragon holds him back by the sleeve.*

1. *hunched* : holding the back and shoulders in a rounded shape.
2. *cringing away* : moving away in fear.
3. *Lucky* : Beckett told Colin Duckworth: 'I suppose he is Lucky to have no more expectations.' (See Duckworth's edition of *En attendant Godot*, p. lxiii.)
4. *stool* : kind of chair without a back.
5. *tautens* [tɔːtənȝ] : tightens.

VLADIMIR. Let me go!

ESTRAGON. Stay where you are!

POZZO. Be careful! He's wicked. *(Vladimir and Estragon turn towards Pozzo.)* With strangers.

ESTRAGON *(undertone)*. Is that him?

VLADIMIR. Who?

ESTRAGON *(trying to remember the name)*. Er...

VLADIMIR. Godot?

ESTRAGON. Yes.

POZZO. I present myself: Pozzo.

VLADIMIR *(to Estragon)*. Not at all!

ESTRAGON. He said Godot.

VLADIMIR. Not at all!

ESTRAGON *(timidly to Pozzo)*. You're not Mr. Godot, sir?

POZZO *(terrifying voice)*. I am Pozzo! *(Silence.)* Pozzo! *(Silence.)* Does that name mean nothing to you? *(Silence)*. I say does that name mean nothing to you?

Vladimir and Estragon look at each other questioningly.

ESTRAGON *(pretending to search)*. Bozzo... Bozzo...

VLADIMIR *(ditto)*. Pozzo... Pozzo...

POZZO. PPPOZZZO!

ESTRAGON. Ah! Pozzo... let me see... Pozzo...

VLADIMIR. It is Pozzo or Bozzo?

ESTRAGON. Pozzo... no... I'm afraid I... no... I don t seem to...

Pozzo advances threateningly.

VLADIMIR *(conciliating)*. I once knew a family called Gozzo. The mother had the clap. [1]

---

1. *the clap* : venereal disease.

ESTRAGON *(hastily).* We're not from these parts, sir.

POZZO *(halting).* You are human beings none the less. *(He puts on his glasses.)* As far as one can see. *(He takes off his glasses.)* Of the same species as myself. *(He bursts into an enormous laugh.)* Of the same species as Pozzo! Made in God's image!

VLADIMIR. Well you see—

POZZO *(peremptory).* Who is Godot?

ESTRAGON. Godot?

POZZO. You took me for Godot.

ESTRAGON. Oh no, sir, not for an instant, sir.

POZZO. Who is he?

VLADIMIR. Oh, he's a... he's a kind of acquaintance.

ESTRAGON. Nothing of the kind, we hardly know him.

VLADIMIR. True... we don't know him very well... but all the same...

ESTRAGON. Personally I wouldn't even know him if I saw him.

POZZO. You took me for him.

ESTRAGON *(recoiling before Pozzo).* That's to say... you understand... the dusk... the strain... waiting... I confess... I imagined... for a second...

POZZO. Waiting? So you were waiting for him?

VLADIMIR. Well you see—

POZZO. Here? On my land?

VLADIMIR. We didn't intend any harm.

ESTRAGON. We meant well.

POZZO. The road is free to all.

VLADIMIR. That's how we looked at it.

POZZO. It's a disgrace. But there you are.

ESTRAGON. Nothing we can do about it.

POZZO *(with magnanimous gesture).* Let's say no more about it. *(He jerks [1] the rope.)* Up pig! *(Pause.)* Every time he drops he falls asleep. *(Jerks the rope.)* Up hog! [2] *(Noise of Lucky getting up and picking up his baggage. Pozzo jerks the rope.)* Back! *(Enter Lucky backwards.)* Stop! *(Lucky stops.)* Turn! *(Lucky turns. To Vladimir and Estragon, affably.)* Gentlemen, I am happy to have met you. *(Before their incredulous expression.)* Yes, yes, sincerely happy. *(He jerks the rope.)* Closer! *(Lucky advances.)* Stop! *(Lucky stops.)* Yes, the road seems long when one journeys all alone for… *(he consults his watch)*… yes… *(he calculates)*… yes, six hours, that's right, six hours on end, and never a soul in sight. *(To Lucky.)* Coat! *(Lucky puts down the bag, advances, gives the coat, goes back to his place, takes up the bag.)* Hold that! *(Pozzo holds out the whip. Lucky advances and, both his hands being occupied, takes the whip in his mouth, then goes back to his place. Pozzo begins to put on his coat, stops.)* Coat! *(Lucky puts down bag, basket and stool, advances, helps Pozzo on with his coat, goes back to his place and takes up bag, basket and stool.)* Touch of autumn in the air this evening. *(Pozzo finishes buttoning his coat, stoops, [3] inspects himself, straightens up.)* Whip! *(Lucky advances, stoops, Pozzo snatches [4] the whip from his mouth, Lucky goes back to his place.)* Yes, gentlemen, I cannot go for long without the society of my likes *(he puts on his glasses and looks at the two likes)* even when the likeness is an imperfect one. *(He takes off his glasses.)* Stool! *(Lucky puts down bag, and basket, advances, opens stool, puts it down, goes back to his place, takes up bag and basket.)* Closer! *(Lucky puts down bag and basket,*

---

1. *jerks* [dʒəːks] : pulls sharply.
2. *hog* : pig.
3. *stoops* : bends down.
4. *snatches* : takes sharply.

*advances, moves stool, goes back to his place, takes up bag
and basket. Pozzo sits down, places the butt [1] of his whip
against Lucky's chest and pushes.)* Back! *(Lucky takes a
step back.)* Further! *(Lucky takes another step back.)* Stop!
(Lucky stops. To Vladimir and Estragon.) That is why,
with your permission, I propose to dally [2] with you a
moment, before I venture any further. Basket! *(Lucky
advances, gives the basket, goes back to his place.)* The
fresh air stimulates the jaded [3] appetite. *(He opens the
basket, takes out a piece of chicken and a bottle of wine.)*
Basket! *(Lucky advances, picks up the basket, goes back to
his place.)* Further! *(Lucky takes a step back.)* He stinks. [4]
Happy days!

*He drinks from the bottle, puts it down and begins to eat.
Silence. Vladimir and Estragon, cautiously at first, then
more boldly, begin to circle about Lucky, inspecting him up
and down. Pozzo eats his chicken voraciously, throwing
away the bones after having sucked them. Lucky sags [5]
slowly, until bag and basket touch the ground, then
straightens up with a start and begins to sag again. Rhythm
of one sleeping on his feet.*

ESTRAGON. What ails him? [6]

VLADIMIR. He looks tired.

ESTRAGON. Why doesn't he put down his bags?

VLADIMIR. How do I know? *(They close in on him.)* Careful!

ESTRAGON. Say something to him.

---

1. *butt* : handle.
2. *dally* ['dạli] : pass the time aimlessly, amuse myself.
3. *jaded* ['dʒeɪdɪd] : tired, lacking zest, usually after too much of
   something.
4. *stinks* : smells unpleasant.
5. *sags* : sinks down.
6. *What ails him?* : What's wrong with him?

VLADIMIR. Look!

ESTRAGON. What?

VLADIMIR *(pointing)*. His neck!

ESTRAGON *(looking at his neck)*. I see nothing.

VLADIMIR. Here.

Estragon goes over beside Vladimir.

ESTRAGON. Oh I say.

VLADIMIR. A running sore!

ESTRAGON. It's the rope.

VLADIMIR. It's the rubbing.

ESTRAGON. It's inevitable.

VLADIMIR. It's the knot.

ESTRAGON. It's the chafing. [1]

They resume their inspection, dwell on the face. [2]

VLADIMIR *(grudgingly)*. [3] He's not bad looking.

ESTRAGON *(shrugging his shoulders,* [4] *wry* [5] *face)*. Would you say so?

VLADIMIR. A trifle effeminate. [6]

ESTRAGON. Look at the slobber. [7]

VLADIMIR. It's inevitable.

ESTRAGON. Look at the slaver! [8]

---

1. *chafing* ['tʃeɪfɪŋ] : irritation from rubbing.
2. *dwell on the face* : remain looking at the face for some time.
3. *grudgingly* ['grʌdzɪŋli] : unwillingly, reluctantly.
4. *shrugging his shoulders* : raising and lowering his shoulders, as if to say he is not sure.
5. *wry* [rʌɪ] : slightly mocking, ironic.
6. *A trifle effeminate* : A little effeminate.
7. *slobber* ['slɒbə] : saliva falling from the mouth.
8. *slaver* ['slavə]: another way of saying slobber.

VLADIMIR. Perhaps he's a half-wit. [1]

ESTRAGON. A cretin.

VLADIMIR *(looking close)*. It looks like a goitre. [2]

ESTRAGON *(ditto)*. It's not certain.

VLADIMIR. He's panting. [3]

ESTRAGON. It's inevitable.

VLADIMIR. And his eyes!

ESTRAGON. What about them?

VLADIMIR. Goggling [4] out of his head.

ESTRAGON. Looks at his last gasp [5] to me.

VLADIMIR. It's not certain. *(Pause.)* Ask him a question.

ESTRAGON. Would that be a good thing?

VLADIMIR. What do we risk?

ESTRAGON *(timidly)*. Mister...

VLADIMIR. Louder.

ESTRAGON *(louder)*. Mister...

POZZO. Leave him in peace! *(They turn towards Pozzo, who, having* *finished eating, wipes his mouth with the back of his hand.)* Can't you see he wants to rest? Basket! *(He strikes a match and begins to light his pipe. Estragon sees the chicken bones on the ground and stares at them greedily. As Lucky does not move Pozzo throws the match angrily away and jerks the rope.)* Basket! *(Lucky starts, almost falls, recovers his senses, advances, puts the bottle in the basket, returns to his place. Estragon stares at the bones.*

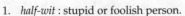

1. *half-wit* : stupid or foolish person.
2. *goitre* ['gɔɪtə] : large swelling of the throat caused by disease of the thyroid gland.
3. *panting* : breathing with short quick breaths.
4. *goggling* ['gɒglɪŋ] : staring with protuberant eyes.
5. *at his last gasp* : near death.

Pozzo strikes another match and lights his pipe.) **What
can you expect, it's not his job.** *(He pulls at his pipe,
stretches out his legs.)* **Ah! That's better.**

ESTRAGON *(timidly).* Please, sir…

POZZO. What is it, my good man?

ESTRAGON. Er… you've finished with the… er… you don't need
the… er… bones, sir?

VLADIMIR *(scandalized).* You couldn't have waited?

POZZO. No no, he does well to ask. Do I need the bones? *(He
turns them over with the end of his whip.)* No, personally
I do not need them any more. *(Estragon takes a step
towards the bones.)* But… *(Estragon stops short)*… but in
theory the bones go to the carrier. He is therefore the
one to ask. *(Estragon turns towards Lucky, hesitates.)* Go
on, go on, don't be afraid, ask him, he'll tell you.

Estragon goes towards Lucky, stops before him.

ESTRAGON. Mister… excuse me, Mister…

POZZO. You're being spoken to, pig! Reply! *(To Estragon.)* Try
him again.

ESTRAGON. Excuse me, Mister, the bones, you won't be wanting
the bones?

Lucky looks long at Estragon.

POZZO *(in raptures).* Mister! *(Lucky bows his head.)* Reply! Do you
want them or don't you? *(Silence of Lucky. To
Estragon.)* They're yours. *(Estragon makes a dart at* [1] *the
bones, picks them up and begins to gnaw* [2] *them.)* I don't
like it. I've never known him refuse a bone before.
(He looks anxiously at Lucky.) Nice business it'd be if he
fell sick on me.

---

1. *makes a dart at* : rushes towards.
2. *gnaw* [nɔː] : chew in the way a dog chews a bone.

He puffs at his pipe.

VLADIMIR *(exploding).* It's a scandal!

Silence. Flabbergasted, [1] *Estragon stops gnawing, looks at Pozzo and Vladimir in turn. Pozzo outwardly calm. Vladimir embarrassed.*

POZZO *(to Vladimir).* Are you alluding to anything in particular?

VLADIMIR *(stutteringly resolute).* [2] To treat a man... *(gesture towards Lucky)*... like that... I think that... no... a human being... no... it's a scandal!

ESTRAGON *(not to be outdone).* [3] A disgrace.

He resumes his gnawing.

POZZO. You are severe. *(To Vladimir.)* What age are you, if it's not a rude question. *(Silence.)* Sixty? Seventy? *(To Estragon.)* What age would you say he was?

ESTRAGON. Eleven.

POZZO. I am impertinent. *(He knocks out his pipe against the whip, gets up.)* I must be getting on. Thank you for your society. *(He reflects.)* Unless I smoke another pipe before I go. What do you say? *(They say nothing.)* Oh I'm only a small smoker, a very small smoker, I'm not in the habit of smoking two pipes one on top of the other, it makes *(hand to heart, sighing)* my heart go pit-a-pat. *(Silence.)* It's the nicotine, one absorbs it in spite of one's precautions. *(Sighs.)* You know how it is. *(Silence.)* But perhaps you don't smoke? Yes? No? It's

1. *flabbergasted* ['flabəgaːstəd] : extremely surprised, stupefied.
2. *stutteringly resolute* ['rɛʒəluːt] : resolute, but with sudden pauses and repetitions in his speech.
3. *not to be outdone* : not wanting to let Vladimir beat him in the competition between them to show which of them can express greater disgust or outrage.

of no importance. *(Silence.)* But how am I to sit down now, without affectation, now that I have risen? Without appearing to—how shall I say—without appearing to falter.[1] *(To Vladimir.)* I beg your pardon? *(Silence.)* Perhaps you didn't speak? *(Silence.)* It's of no importance. Let me see...

He reflects.

ESTRAGON. Ah! That's better.

He puts the bones in his pocket.

VLADIMIR. Let's go.

ESTRAGON. So soon?

POZZO. One moment. *(He jerks the rope.)* Stool! *(He points with his whip. Lucky moves the stool.)* More! There! *(He sits down. Lucky goes back to his place.)* Done it!

He fills his pipe.

VLADIMIR *(vehemently)*. Let's go!

POZZO. I hope I'm not driving you away. Wait a little longer, you'll never regret it.

ESTRAGON *(scenting charity)*. We're in no hurry.

POZZO *(having lit his pipe)*. The second is never so sweet... *(he takes the pipe out of his mouth, contemplates it)*... as the first, I mean. *(He puts the pipe back in his mouth.)* But it's sweet just the same.

VLADIMIR. I'm going.

POZZO. He can no longer endure my presence. I am perhaps not particularly human, but who cares? *(To Vladimir.)* Think twice before you do anything rash.[2] Suppose

---

1. *falter* ['fɔːltə] : move hesitantly.
2. *rash* : impetuous.

you go now, while it is still day, for there is no denying it is still day. *(They all look up at the sky.)* Good. *(They stop looking at the sky.)* What happens in that case—*(he takes the pipe out of his mouth, examines it)*—I'm out—*(he relights his pipe)*—in that case—*(puff)*—in that case—*(puff)*—what happens in that case to your appointment with this... Godet... Godot... Godin... anyhow you see who I mean, who has your future in his hands... *(pause)*... at least your immediate future.

VLADIMIR. Who told you?

POZZO. He speaks to me again! If this goes on much longer we'll soon be old friends.

ESTRAGON. Why doesn't he put down his bags?

POZZO. I too would be happy to meet him. The more people I meet the happier I become. From the meanest creature one departs wiser, richer, more conscious of one's blessings. Even you... *(he looks at them ostentatiously in turn to make it clear they are both meant)*... even you, who knows, will have added to my store.

ESTRAGON. Why doesn't he put down his bags?

POZZO. But that would surprise me.

VLADIMIR. You're being asked a question.

POZZO *(delighted)*. A question! Who? What? A moment ago you were calling me sir, in fear and trembling. Now you're asking me questions. No good will come of this!

VLADIMIR *(to Estragon)*. I think he's listening.

ESTRAGON *(circling about Lucky)*. What?

VLADIMIR. You can ask him now. He's on the alert.

ESTRAGON. Ask him what?

VLADIMIR. Why he doesn't put down his bags.

ESTRAGON. I wonder.

VLADIMIR. Ask him, can't you?

POZZO *(who has followed these exchanges with anxious attention, fearing lest* [1] *the question get lost).* You want to know why he doesn't put down his bags, as you call them?

VLADIMIR. That's it.

POZZO *(to Estragon).* You are sure you agree with that?

ESTRAGON. He's puffing like a grampus. [2]

POZZO. The answer is this. *(To Estragon.)* But stay still, I beg of you, you're making me nervous!

VLADIMIR. Here.

ESTRAGON. What is it?

VLADIMIR. He's about to speak.

> *Estragon goes over beside Vladimir.*
> *Motionless, side by side, they wait.*

POZZO. Good. Is everybody ready? Is everybody looking at me? *(He looks at Lucky, jerks the rope. Lucky raises his head.)* Will you look at me, pig! *(Lucky looks at him.)* Good. *(He puts his pipe in his pocket, takes out a little vaporizer and sprays his throat,* [3] *puts back the vaporizer in his pocket, clears his throat, spits, takes out the vaporizer again, sprays his throat again, puts back the vaporizer in his pocket.)* I am ready. Is everybody listening? Is everybody ready? *(He looks at them all in turn, jerks the*

---

1. *lest* : in case.
2. *puffing like a grampus* : breathing noisily. A grampus is a large dolphin-like sea animal. This is an informal idiomatic expression.
3. *sprays his throat* : Entertainers, particularly singers, used sprays to clear their throats before going on stage. Pozzo, it is clear, intends to give a performance. This is one of the many points where Beckett draws attention to the fact that we are watching a theatrical event. The attempt at illusion of the traditional theatre is deliberately undermined.

rope.) Hog! *(Lucky raises his head.)* I don't like talking in a vacuum. Good. Let me see.

He reflects.

ESTRAGON. I'm going.

POZZO. What was it exactly you wanted to know?

VLADIMIR. Why he—

POZZO *(angrily).* Don't interrupt me! *(Pause. Calmer.)* If we all speak at once we'll never get anywhere. *(Pause.)* What was I saying? *(Pause. Louder.)* What was I saying?

Vladimir mimics one carrying a heavy burden. Pozzo looks at him, puzzled.

ESTRAGON *(forcibly).* Bags. *(He points at Lucky.)* Why? Always hold. *(He sags, panting.)* Never put down. *(He opens his hands, straightens up with relief.)* Why?

POZZO. Ah! Why couldn't you say so before? Why he doesn't make himself comfortable? Let's try and get it clear. Has he not the right to? Certainly he has. It follows that he doesn't want to. There's reasoning for you. And why doesn't he want to? *(Pause.)* Gentlemen, the reason is this.

VLADIMIR *(to Estragon).* Make a note of this.

POZZO. He wants to impress me, so that I'll keep him.

ESTRAGON. What?

POZZO. Perhaps I haven't got it quite right. He wants to mollify [1] me, so that I'll give up the idea of parting with him. No, that's not exactly it either.

VLADIMIR. You want to get rid of him?

POZZO. He wants to cod me, [2] but he won't.

---

1. *mollify me* : soothe me, make me calmer.
2. *cod me* : fool me, deceive me – an Irish expression.

VLADIMIR. You want to get rid of him?

POZZO. He imagines that when I see how well he carries I'll be tempted to keep him on in that capacity.

ESTRAGON. You've had enough of him?

POZZO. In reality he carries like a pig. It's not his job.

VLADIMIR. You want to get rid of him?

POZZO. He imagines that when I see him indefatigable I'll regret my decision. Such is his miserable scheme. As though I were short of slaves! *(All three look at Lucky.)* Atlas, son of Jupiter! [1] *(Silence.)* Well, that's that I think. Anything else? Vaporizer.

VLADIMIR. You want to get rid of him?

POZZO. Remark that I might just as well have been in his shoes and he in mine. If chance had not willed otherwise. To each one his due.

VLADIMIR. You waagerrim? [2]

POZZO. I beg your pardon?

VLADIMIR. You want to get rid of him?

POZZO. I do. But instead of driving him away as I might have done, I mean instead of simply kicking him out on his arse, [3] in the goodness of my heart I am bringing him to the fair, where I hope to get a good price for him. The truth is you can't drive such creatures away. The best thing would be to kill them.

Lucky weeps.

ESTRAGON. He's crying.

---

1. *son of Jupiter* : Pozzo is mistaken: Atlas was the son of the Titan, Iapetus.

2. *waagerrim* : Vladimir speaks very quickly and unclearly: 'want to get rid of him'.

3. *arse* : vulgar word for buttocks.

POZZO. Old dogs have more dignity. *(He proffers his handkerchief to Estragon.)* Comfort him, since you pity him. *(Estragon hesitates.)* Come on. *(Estragon takes the handkerchief.)* Wipe away his tears, he'll feel less forsaken. [1]

Estragon hesitates.

VLADIMIR. Here, give it to me, I'll do it.

Estragon refuses to give the handkerchief. Childish gestures.

POZZO. Make haste, before he stops. *(Estragon approaches Lucky and makes to wipe his eyes. Lucky kicks him violently in the shins. [2] Estragon drops the handkerchief, recoils, staggers about the stage with pain.)*
Hanky!
Lucky puts down bag and basket, picks up handkerchief, gives it to Pozzo, goes back to his place, picks up bag and basket.

ESTRAGON. Oh the swine! *(He pulls up the leg of his trousers.)* He's crippled me! [3]

POZZO. I told you he didn't like strangers.

VLADIMIR *(to Estragon).* Show. *(Estragon shows his leg. To Pozzo, angrily.)* He's bleeding!

POZZO. It's a good sign.

ESTRAGON *(on one leg).* I'll never walk again!

VLADIMIR *(tenderly).* I'll carry you. *(Pause.)* If necessary.

POZZO. He's stopped crying. *(To Estragon.)* You have replaced him as it were. *(Lyrically.)* The tears of the world are a constant quantity. For each one who begins to weep, somewhere else another stops. The same is true of the laugh. *(He laughs.)* Let us not then speak ill of our

---

1. *forsaken* [fə'seɪkən] : abandoned.
2. *shin(s)* : front of leg below knee.
3. *crippled me* ['krɪpəld] : damaged me seriously, made me lame.

generation, it is not any unhappier than its predecessors. *(Pause.)* Let us not speak well of it either. *(Pause.)* Let us not speak of it at all. *(Pause. Judiciously.)* It is true the population has increased.

VLADIMIR. Try and walk.

Estragon takes a few limping steps, [1] *stops before Lucky and spits on him, then goes and sits down on the mound.*

POZZO. Guess who taught me all these beautiful things. *(Pause. Pointing to Lucky.)* My Lucky!

VLADIMIR *(looking at the sky)*. Will night never come?

POZZO. But for him all my thoughts, all my feelings, would have been of common things. *(Pause. With extraordinary vehemence.)* Professional worries! *(Calmer.)* Beauty, grace, truth of the first water, I knew they were all beyond me. So I took a knook. [2]

VLADIMIR *(startled from his inspection of the sky)*. A knook?

POZZO. That was nearly sixty years ago... *(he consults his watch)*... yes, nearly sixty. *(Drawing himself up proudly.)* You wouldn't think it to look at me, would you? Compared to him I look like a young man, no? *(Pause.)* Hat! *(Lucky puts down the basket and takes off his hat. His long white hair falls about his face. He puts his hat under his arm and picks up the basket.)* Now look. *(Pozzo takes off his hat. He is completely bald. He puts on his hat again.)* Did you see?

VLADIMIR. And now you turn him away? Such an old and faithful servant.

ESTRAGON. Swine!

Pozzo more and more agitated.

---

1. *limping steps* : steps made difficult by the injury to his leg.
2. *knook* : A word invented by Beckett: it was suggested by the word for a Russian whip, knout.

VLADIMIR. After having sucked all the good out of him you chuck
    him away [1] like a... like a banana skin. Really...

POZZO *(groaning, clutching* [2] *his head).* I can't bear it... any
    longer... the way he goes on... you've no idea... it's
    terrible... he must go... *(he waves his arms)...* I'm
    going mad... *(he collapses, his head in his hands)...* I
    can't bear it... any longer...

    Silence. All look at Pozzo.

VLADIMIR. He can't bear it.

ESTRAGON. Any longer.

VLADIMIR. He's going mad.

ESTRAGON. It's terrible.

VLADIMIR *(to Lucky).* How dare you! It's abominable! Such a good
    master! Crucify him like that! After so many years!
    Really!

POZZO *(sobbing).* He used to be so kind... so helpful... and
    entertaining... my good angel... and now... he's
    killing me.

ESTRAGON *(to Vladimir).* Does he want to replace him?

VLADIMIR. What?

ESTRAGON. Does he want someone to take his place or not?

VLADIMIR. I don't think so.

ESTRAGON. What?

VLADIMIR. I don't know.

ESTRAGON. Ask him.

POZZO *(calmer).* Gentlemen, I don't know what came over me.
    Forgive me. Forget all I said. *(More and more his old
    self.)* I don't remember exactly what it was, but you

---

1. *chuck him away* : throw him away, discard him.
2. *clutching* : holding tightly.

may be sure there wasn't a word of truth in it. *(Drawing himself up, striking his chest.)* Do I look like a man that can be made to suffer? Frankly? *(He rummages in his pockets.)* What have I done with my pipe?

VLADIMIR. Charming evening we're having.

ESTRAGON. Unforgettable.

VLADIMIR. And it's not over.

ESTRAGON. Apparently not.

VLADIMIR. It's only beginning.

ESTRAGON. It's awful.

VLADIMIR. Worse than the pantomime.

ESTRAGON. The circus.

VLADIMIR. The music-hall.

ESTRAGON. The circus.

POZZO. What can I have done with that briar? [1]

ESTRAGON. He's a scream. [2] He's lost his dudeen. [3]

Laughs noisily.

VLADIMIR. I'll be back.

He hastens towards the wings.

ESTRAGON. End of the corridor, on the left.

VLADIMIR. Keep my seat.

Exit Vladimir.

1. *briar* : pipe; refers to the wood from which pipes are made.
2. *a scream* : something so funny that it makes people scream with laughter.
3. *dudeen* : the Irish word for a clay pipe (used only in Ireland).

POZZO. I've lost my Kapp and Peterson![1]

ESTRAGON (*convulsed with merriment*). He'll be the death of me!

POZZO (*looking up*). You didn't by any chance see—(*He misses Vladimir.*) Oh! He's gone! Without saying good-bye! How could he! He might have waited!

ESTRAGON. He would have burst.

POZZO. Oh! (*Pause.*) Oh well then of course in that case...

ESTRAGON. Come here.

POZZO. What for?

ESTRAGON. You'll see.

POZZO. You want me to get up?

ESTRAGON. Quick! (*Pozzo gets up and goes over beside Estragon. Estragon points off.*) Look!

POZZO (*having put on his glasses*). Oh I say!

ESTRAGON. It's all over.

> *Enter Vladimir, sombre. He shoulders Lucky out of his way, kicks over the stool, comes and goes agitatedly.*

POZZO. He's not pleased.

ESTRAGON (*to Vladimir*). You missed a treat.[2] Pity.

> *Vladimir halts, straightens the stool, comes and goes, calmer.*

POZZO. He subsides. (*Looking round.*) Indeed all subsides. A great calm descends. (*Raising his hand.*) Listen! Pan sleeps.[3]

---

1. *Kapp and Peterson* : A make of Irish pipe.
2. *treat* : special and pleasant experience, often a reward for good behaviour.
3. *Pan sleeps* : Pozzo is evidently fond of mythological illusions. This, his second, refers to the Greek god of flocks and herds. Pan's appearance was dreaded by travellers, whom he startled, arousing panic and fear. The word pan, in Greek, means 'all', and Pan came to be regarded as the personification of Nature or the Universe, to whom Socrates prayed for beauty of soul. The reference to Pan, then, produces ironic resonances.

VLADIMIR. Will night never come?

All three look at the sky.

POZZO. You don't feel like going until it does?

ESTRAGON. Well you see—

POZZO. Why it's very natural, very natural. I myself in your situation, if I had an appointment with a Godin… Godet… Godot… anyhow, you see who I mean, I'd wait till it was black night before I gave up. *(He looks at the stool.)* I'd like very much to sit down, but I don't quite know how to go about it.

ESTRAGON. Could I be of any help?

POZZO. If you asked me perhaps.

ESTRAGON. What?

POZZO. If you asked me to sit down.

ESTRAGON. Would that be a help?

POZZO. I fancy so.

ESTRAGON. Here we go. Be seated, sir, I beg of you.

POZZO. No, no, I wouldn't think of it! *(Pause. Aside.)* Ask me again.

ESTRAGON. Come come, take a seat, I beseech [1] you, you'll get pneumonia.

POZZO. You really think so?

ESTRAGON. Why it's absolutely certain.

POZZO. No doubt you are right. *(He sits down.)* Done it again! *(Pause.)* Thank you, dear fellow. *(He consults his watch.)* But I must really be getting along, if I am to observe my schedule.

VLADIMIR. Time has stopped.

---

1. *beseech* [bɪ'siːtʃ] : pray, beg.

POZZO *(cuddling his watch to his ear)*. Don't you believe it, sir, don't you believe it. *(He puts his watch back in his pocket.)* Whatever you like, but not that.

ESTRAGON *(to Pozzo)*. Everything seems black to him today.

POZZO. Except the firmament! *(He laughs, pleased with this witticism.)* But I see what it is, you are not from these parts, you don't know what our twilights can do. Shall I tell you? *(Silence. Estragon is fiddling with his boot again, Vladimir with his hat.)* I can't refuse you. *(Vaporizer.)* A little attention, if you please. *(Vladimir and Estragon continue their fiddling,* [1] *Lucky is half asleep. Pozzo cracks his whip* [2] *feebly.)* [3] What's the matter with this whip? *(He gets up and cracks it more vigorously, finally with success. Lucky jumps. Vladimir's hat, Estragon's boot, Lucky's hat, fall to the ground. Pozzo throws down the whip.)* Worn out, this whip. *(He looks at Vladimir and Estragon.)* What was I saying?

VLADIMIR. Let's go.

ESTRAGON. But take the weight off your feet, I implore you, you'll catch your death.

POZZO. True. *(He sits down. To Estragon.)* What is your name?

ESTRAGON. Adam.

POZZO *(who hasn't listened)*. Ah, yes! The night. *(He raises his head.)* But be a little more attentive, for pity's sake, otherwise we'll never get anywhere. *(He looks at the sky.)* Look. *(All look at the sky except Lucky who is dozing off* [4] *again. Pozzo jerks the rope.)* Will you look at the sky, pig! *(Lucky looks at the sky.)* Good, that's enough. *(They stop looking at the sky.)* What is there so

1. *fiddling* : playing aimlessly.
2. *cracks his whip* : causes his whip to make a sharp sound.
3. *feebly* : weakly.
4. *dozing* [dəʊʒiŋ] *off* : falling asleep.

extraordinary about it? Qua sky. [1] It is pale and luminous like any sky at this hour of the day. *(Pause.)* In these latitudes. *(Pause.)* When the weather is fine. *(Lyrical.)* An hour ago *(he looks at this watch, prosaic)* roughly *(lyrical)* after having poured forth ever since *(he hesitates, prosaic)* say ten o'clock in the morning *(lyrical)* tirelessly torrents of red and white light it begins to lose its effulgence, [2] to grow pale *(gesture of the two hands lapsing [3] by stages)*, pale, ever a little paler, a little paler until *(dramatic pause, ample gesture of the two hands flung wide apart)* pppfff! finished! it comes to rest. But—*(hand raised in admonition)*—but behind this veil of gentleness and peace night is charging *(vibrantly)* and will burst upon us *(snaps his fingers)* pop! like that! *(his inspiration leaves him)* just when we least expect it. *(Silence. Gloomily.)* That's how it is on this bitch of an earth.

Long silence.

ESTRAGON. So long as one knows.

VLADIMIR. One can bide [4] one's time.

ESTRAGON. One knows what to expect.

VLADIMIR. No further need to worry.

ESTRAGON. Simply wait.

VLADIMIR. We're used to it. He picks up his hat, looks inside it, shakes it, puts it on.

POZZO. How did you find me? *(Vladimir and Estragon look at him blankly.)* Good? Fair? Middling? Poor? Positively bad?

VLADIMIR *(first to understand)*. Oh very good, very very good.

---

1. *Qua sky* : as sky.
2. *effulgence* : radiance, brilliance.
3. *lapsing* : falling away, growing smaller.
4. *bide* : wait.

POZZO *(to Estragon).* And you, sir?

ESTRAGON. Oh tray bong, tray tray tray bong. [1]

POZZO *(fervently).* Bless you, gentlemen, bless you! *(Pause.)* I have such need of encouragement! *(Pause.)* I weakened a little towards the end, you didn't notice?

VLADIMIR. Oh perhaps just a teeny weeny little bit. [2]

ESTRAGON. I thought it was intentional.

POZZO. You see my memory is defective.

  Silence.

ESTRAGON. In the meantime nothing happens.

POZZO. You find it tedious?

ESTRAGON. Somewhat.

POZZO *(to Vladimir).* And you, sir?

VLADIMIR. I've been better entertained.

  Silence. Pozzo struggles inwardly.

POZZO. Gentlemen, you have been… civil to me.

ESTRAGON. Not at all.

VLADIMIR. What an idea!

POZZO. Yes yes, you have been correct. So that I ask myself is there anything I can do in my turn for these honest fellows who are having such a dull, dull time.

ESTRAGON. Even ten francs would be welcome.

VLADIMIR. We are not beggars!

POZZO. Is there anything I can do, that's what I ask myself, to cheer them up? I have given them bones, I have

---

1. *Oh tray bong, tray tray tray bong* : Estragon's anglicised pronunciation of *très bon*.
2. *teeny weeny little bit* : very, very small amount.

talked to them about this and that, I have explained the twilight, admittedly. But is it enough, that's what tortures me, is it enough?

ESTRAGON. Even five.

VLADIMIR *(to Estragon, indignantly)*. That's enough!

ESTRAGON. I couldn't accept less.

POZZO. Is it enough? No doubt. But I am liberal. It's my nature. This evening. So much the worse for me. *(He jerks the rope. Lucky looks at him.)* For I shall suffer, no doubt about that. *(He picks up the whip.)* What do you prefer? Shall we have him dance, or sing, or recite, or think, or—

ESTRAGON. Who?

POZZO. Who! You know how to think, you two?

VLADIMIR. He thinks?

POZZO. Certainly. Aloud. He even used to think very prettily once, I could listen to him for hours. Now… *(he shudders).* [1] So much the worse for me. Well, would you like him to think something for us?

ESTRAGON. I'd rather he'd dance, it'd be more fun?

POZZO. Not necessarily.

ESTRAGON. Wouldn't it, Didi, be more fun?

VLADIMIR. I'd like well to hear him think.

ESTRAGON. Perhaps he could dance first and think afterwards, if it isn't too much to ask him.

VLADIMIR *(to Pozzo)*. Would that be possible?

POZZO. By all means, nothing simpler. It's the natural order.

He laughs briefly.

VLADIMIR. Then let him dance.

---

1. *shudders* : shakes violently with horror.

Silence.

POZZO. Do you hear, hog?

ESTRAGON. He never refuses?

POZZO. He refused once. *(Silence.)* Dance, misery!

> *Lucky puts down basket, advances towards front, turns to Pozzo. Lucky dances. He stops.*

ESTRAGON. Is that all?

POZZO. Encore!

> *Lucky executes the same movements, stops.*

ESTRAGON. Pooh! I'd do as well myself. *(He imitates Lucky, almost falls.)* With a little practice.

POZZO. He used to dance the farandole, the fling, the brawl, the jig, the fandango, and even the hornpipe. [1] He capered. For joy. Now that's the best he can do. Do you know what he calls it? [2]

ESTRAGON. The Scapegoat's [3] Agony.

VLADIMIR. The Hard Stool. [4]

POZZO. The Net. He thinks he's entangled in a net.

VLADIMIR *(squirming [5] like an aesthete)*. There's something about it…

---

1. *the farandole, etc.* : traditional dances.
2. *Do you know what he calls it?* There is no doubt, on the basis of his director's notes, that Beckett intended Lucky's dance as a metaphor for human existence.
3. *Scapegoat* : person who is blamed or punished for the wrongdoing of others.
4. *The Hard Stool* : The Hard Faeces, presumably comparing Lucky's movements in his dance to the straining to excrete of a person with constipation. His movements are stiff, lack fluidity. Beckett uses 'the iron stool' in the same way in *Krapp's Last Tape*.
5. *squirming* [skwəːmɪŋ] : twisting the body about, writhing.

Lucky makes to return to his burdens. [1]

POZZO. Woaa!

Lucky stiffens.

ESTRAGON. Tell us about the time he refused.

POZZO. With pleasure, with pleasure. *(He fumbles* [2] *in his pockets.)* Wait. *(He fumbles.)* What have I done with my spray? *(He fumbles.)* Well now isn't that... *(He looks up, consternation on his features. Faintly.)* I can't find my pulverizer! [3]

ESTRAGON *(faintly).* My left lung is very weak! *(He coughs feebly. In ringing tones.)* But my right lung is as sound as a bell!

POZZO *(normal voice).* No matter! What was I saying. *(He ponders.)* Wait. *(Ponders.)* Well now isn't that... *(He raises his head).* Help me!

ESTRAGON. Wait!

VLADIMIR. Wait!

POZZO. Wait!

All three take off their hats simultaneously, press their hands to their foreheads, concentrate.

ESTRAGON *(triumphantly).* Ah!

VLADIMIR. He has it.

POZZO *(impatient).* Well?

ESTRAGON. Why doesn't he put down his bags?

VLADIMIR. Rubbish!

POZZO. Are you sure?

---

1. *burdens* ['bɔːdənʒ] : things to be carried, heavy loads.
2. *fumbles* ['fʌmbəlʒ] : searches clumsily.
3. *pulverizer* ['pʌlvərʌizə] : device used to divide liquid into spray: Pozzo's vaporizer.

VLADIMIR. Damn it, Haven't you already told us!

POZZO. I've already told you?

ESTRAGON. He's already told us?

VLADIMIR. Anyway he has put them down.

ESTRAGON (*glance at Lucky*). So he has. And what of it?

VLADIMIR. Since he has put down his bags it is impossible we should have asked why he does not do so.

POZZO. Stoutly [1] reasoned!

ESTRAGON. And why has he put them down?

POZZO. Answer us that.

VLADIMIR. In order to dance.

ESTRAGON. True!

POZZO. True!

> *Silence. They put on their hats.*

ESTRAGON. Nothing happens, nobody comes, nobody goes, it's awful!

VLADIMIR (*to Pozzo*). Tell him to think.

POZZO. Give him his hat.

VLADIMIR. His hat?

POZZO. He can't think without his hat.

VLADIMIR (*to Estragon*). Give him his hat.

ESTRAGON. Me! After what he did to me! Never!

VLADIMIR. I'll give it to him.

> *He does not move.*

ESTRAGON (*to Pozzo*). Tell him to go and fetch it.

POZZO. It's better to give it to him.

VLADIMIR. I'll give it to him.

1. *stoutly* : soundly, sensibly.

He picks up the hat and tenders [1] *it at arm's length to Lucky, who does not move.*

POZZO. You must put it on his head.

ESTRAGON *(to Pozzo).* Tell him to take it.

POZZO. It's better to put it on his head.

VLADIMIR. I'll put it on his head.

He goes round behind Lucky, approaches him cautiously, puts the hat on his head and recoils [2] *smartly. Lucky does not move. Silence.*

ESTRAGON. What's he waiting for?

POZZO. Stand back! *(Vladimir and Estragon move away from Lucky. Pozzo jerks the rope. Lucky looks at Pozzo.)* Think, pig! *(Pause. Lucky begins to dance.)* Stop! *(Lucky stops.)* Forward! *(Lucky advances.)* Stop! *(Lucky stops.)* Think!

Silence.

LUCKY. On the other hand with regard to—

POZZO. Stop! *(Lucky stops.)* Back! *(Lucky moves back.)* Stop! *(Lucky stops.)* Turn! *(Lucky turns towards auditorium.)* Think!

During Lucky's tirade the others react as follows: (1) Vladimir and Estragon all attention, Pozzo dejected and disgusted. (2) Vladimir and Estragon begin to protest, Pozzo's sufferings increase. (3) Vladimir and Estragon attentive again, Pozzo more and more agitated and groaning. (4) Vladimir and Estragon protest violently. Pozzo jumps up, pulls on the rope. General outcry. Lucky pulls on the rope, staggers, shouts his text. All three throw themselves on Lucky who struggles and shouts his text.

---

1. *tenders* : offers.
2. *recoils* : moves back, withdraws.

LUCKY. Given the existence [1] as uttered forth in the public works
        of Puncher [2] and Wattmann [3] of a personal God
        quaquaquaqua [4] with white beard quaquaquaqua
        outside time without extension who from the heights
        of divine apathia [5] divine athambia [6] divine aphasia [7]
        loves us dearly with some exceptions for reasons
        unknown but time will tell and suffers like the divine
        Miranda [8] with those who for reasons unknown but

1. *Given the existence...* : In the diary kept by Walter Asmus,
   Beckett's co-director at the Schiller Theatre (in D. McMillan & M.
   Fehsenfeld, *Beckett in the Theatre*, pp. 136 -148), there is the
   following explanation by Beckett of Lucky's monologue (p. 138):
   'It is not as difficult as it may seem. It will be divided into three
   parts and the second part is going to be divided again into two
   sections. The first part is about the indifference of heaven, about
   divine apathy. This part ends with, 'but not so fast...' The second
   part starts off with 'considering what is more', and is about man,
   who is shrinking – about man, who is dwindling. Not only the
   dwindling is important here, but the shrinking, too. These two
   points represent the two under-sections of the second part. The
   theme of the third part is 'the earth abode of stones' and starts
   with 'considering what is more, much more grave.''

2. *Puncher* : ticket-puncher.

3. *Wattmann* : Duckworth (op. cit., p.cvii) explains: 'a tram-driver
   who cannot go off the rails laid down for him.' Puncher and
   Wattmann are non-existent philosophers or theologians (experts
   on the nature of God). In the second name there seems to be a
   pun on 'What man?'

4. *quaquaquaqua* : in Beckett's manuscript *quoique*, which means
   'although'. Beckett offered the suggestion to the writers of *A
   Student's Guide to the Plays of Samuel Beckett* (B. Fletcher and
   others): 'quaquaversal: divine attribute'. 'Quaquaversal' means
   'pointing in every direction'. 'Quaqua' also suggests the noise
   made by a duck (quack quack), a meaningless sound.

5. *apathia* [æ'pəθɪə] : insensibility to suffering.

6. *athambia* [æθæmbɪə] : imperturbability.

7. *aphasia* [ə'feɪzɪə] : inability to express thought in words, or
   inability to understand thought as expressed in words by others.

8. *Miranda* : the daughter of Prospero, the principal character in
   Shakespeare's *The Tempest*.

time will tell are plunged in torment plunged in fire whose fire flames if that continues and who can doubt it will fire the firmament that is to say blast hell to heaven so blue still and calm[1] so calm with a calm which even though intermittent is better than nothing but not so fast and considering what is more that as a result of the labours left unfinished crowned by the Acacacacademy of Anthropopopometry[2] of Essy-in-Possy[3] of Testew[4] and Cunard it is established beyond all doubt all other doubt than that which clings to the labours of men that as a result of the labours unfinished of Testew and Cunard it is established as hereinafter but not so fast for reasons unknown that as a result of the public works of Puncher and Wattmann it is established beyond all doubt that in view of the labours of Fartov and Belcher left unfinished for reasons unknown of Testew and Cunard left unfinished it is established what many deny that man in Possy of Testew and

1. *heaven so blue still and calm* : A disguised quotation from Verlaine's 'Le Ciel', in *Sagesse*.

2. *Acacacacademy of Anthropopopometry* : Duckworth (op. cit., p.cvii) says that Lucky revels 'in names concocted with Rabelaisian irreverence out of the private parts and the excretive functions'. Caca is used by French children to mean excrement (it is also used in the same way by Italian children, and also in South Wales, where it is spelt 'cacka', with the adjectival form 'cacky'); 'po' is a colloquialism for chamber-pot. *Anthropometry*: man-measurement (an invented word).

3. *Essy-in-Possy* : deliberate corruptions of Latin esse 'to be' and posse 'to be able'.

4. *Testew, Cunard, Fartov, Belcher* : all words of vulgar derivation (testes, cunt, fart, belch). 'Cunt' is a demotic word for the female genitals; to fart or to let off a fart is to emit wind from the anus; to belch is to emit wind noisily from the stomach through the mouth. There may also be a reference to Nancy Cunard, whose Hours Press published the poem 'Whoroscope', Beckett's first published work, in 1930.

Cunard that man in Essy that man in short that man
in brief in spite of the strides of alimentation and
defecation is seen to waste and pine [1] waste and pine
and concurrently simultaneously what is more for
reasons unknown in spite of the strides of physical
culture the practice of sports such as tennis football
running cycling swimming flying floating riding
gliding conating [2] camogie [3] skating tennis of all kinds
dying flying sports of all sorts autumn summer
winter winter tennis of all kinds hockey of all sorts
penicilline and succedanea [4] in a word I resume and
concurrently simultaneously for reasons unknown to
shrink and dwindle [5] in spite of the tennis I resume
flying gliding golf over nine and eighteen holes
tennis of all sorts in a word for reasons unknown in
Feckham Peckham Fulham Clapham [6] namely
concurrently simultaneously what is more for reasons
unknown but time will tell to shrink and dwindle I
resume Fulham Clapham in a word the dead loss per
caput since the death of Bishop Berkeley [7] being to the

1. *pine* : languish, waste away, from grief.

2. *conating* [kə'neɪtɪŋ] : desiring to perform an action.

3. *camogie* : an Irish form of women's hockey.

4. *succedanea* : substitutes.

5. *shrink and dwindle* : two ways of saying 'grow smaller'.

6. *Feckham, Peckham, Fulham, Clapham* : The first name is invented,
    while the other three are real places in London.

7. *Bishop Berkeley* : an Irish philosopher (1685 – 1753) admired by
    Beckett. Berkeley arrived at the conclusion that the only solution to
    the philosophical perplexities of his time in relation to the defining
    of reality was to deny the existence of *matter*. His doctrine was 'of a
    wholly non-material, theocentric universe, whose *esse* was *percipi*,
    and in which human 'spirits' were conceived of as conversing
    directly with the mind of God.' (*The Oxford Companion to
    Philosophy*, ed. Ted Honderich, p. 91.) 'Berkeley's . . . thesis is
    encapsulated in the motto *esse est percipi*: for unthinking things, to
    exist is none other than to be perceived.' (*The Oxford Illustrated
    History of Western Philosophy*, p. 142)

tune of one inch four ounce per caput approximately
by and large more or less to the nearest decimal good
measure round figures stark naked in the stockinged
feet in Connemara in a word for reasons unknown no
matter what matter the facts are there and
considering what is more much more grave that in
the light of the labours lost [1] of Steinweg and
Peterman [2] it appears what is more much more grave
that in the light the light the light of the labours lost
of Steinweg and Peterman that in the plains in the
mountains by the seas by the rivers running water
running fire the air is the same and then the earth
namely the air and then the earth in the great cold the
great dark the air and the earth abode of stones in the
great cold alas alas in the year of their Lord six
hundred and something the air the earth the sea the
earth abode of stones in the great deeps the great cold
on sea on land and in the air I resume for reasons
unknown in spite of the tennis the facts are there but
time will tell I resume alas alas on on in short in fine
on on abode of stones who can doubt it I resume but
not so fast I resume the skull to shrink and waste and
concurrently simultaneously what is more for reasons
unknown in spite of the tennis On on the beard the
flames the tears the stones so blue so calm alas alas
on on the skull the skull the skull the skull in
Connemara [3] in spite of the tennis the labours
abandoned left unfinished graver still abode of stones
in a word I resume alas alas abandoned unfinished

1. *labours lost* : refers to Shakespeare's *Love's Labour's Lost*.

2. *Steinweg and Peterman* : invented names, each of which includes
   an element referring to stones *(stein, Peter)* – note 'the earth
   abode of stones' which follows a little later.

3. *the skull in Connemara* : possibly a reference to the death of
   Thelma, wife of Beckett's first fictional hero, Belacqua (*More
   Pricks than Kicks*, p. 189).

the skull the skull in Connemara in spite of the tennis the skull alas the stones Cunard *(mêlée, final vociferations)* tennis... the stones... so calm... Cunard... unfinished...

POZZO. His hat!

Vladimir seizes Lucky's hat. Silence of Lucky. He falls. Silence. Panting of the victors.

ESTRAGON. Avenged!

Vladimir examines the hat, peers inside it.

POZZO. Give me that! *(He snatches the hat from Vladimir, throws it on the ground, tramples on* [1] *it.)* There's an end to his thinking!

VLADIMIR. But will he be able to walk?

POZZO. Walk or crawl! *(He kicks Lucky.)* Up pig!

ESTRAGON. Perhaps he's dead.

VLADIMIR. You'll kill him.

POZZO. Up scum! [2] *(He jerks the rope.)* Help me!

VLADIMIR. How?

POZZO. Raise him up!

Vladimir and Estragon hoist [3] *Lucky to his feet, support him an instant, then let him go. He falls.*

ESTRAGON. He's doing it on purpose!

POZZO. You must hold him. *(Pause.)* Come on, come on, raise him up!

ESTRAGON. To hell with him!

1. *tramples* ['trampəls] *on* : crushes by treading on.
2. *scum* : contemptible object (scum means a layer of dirt on a pond or other area of still water).
3. *hoist* : lift with effort.

VLADIMIR. Come on, once more.

ESTRAGON. What does he take us for?

They raise Lucky, hold him up.

POZZO. Don't let him go! *(Vladimir and Estragon totter.)* [1] Don't
    move! *(Pozzo fetches bag and basket and brings them
    towards Lucky.)* Hold him tight! *(He puts the bag in
    Lucky's hand. Lucky drops it immediately.)* Don't let him
    go! *(He puts back the bag in Lucky's hand. Gradually, at
    the feel of the bag, Lucky recovers his senses and his fingers
    close round the handle.)* Hold him tight! *(As before with
    basket.)* Now! You can let him go. *(Vladimir and
    Estragon move away from Lucky, who totters, reels,* [2]
    sags, [3] *but succeeds in remaining on his feet, bag and
    basket in his hands. Pozzo steps back, cracks his whip.)*
    Forward! *(Lucky totters forward.)* Back! *(Lucky totters
    back.)* Turn! *(Lucky turns.)* Done it! He can walk.
    (Turning towards Vladimir and Estragon.) Thank you
    gentlemen, and let me... *(he fumbles in his pockets)*...
    let me wish you... *(fumbles)*... wish you... *(fumbles)*...
    what have I done with my watch? *(Fumbles.)* A
    genuine half-hunter, [4] gentlemen, with deadbeat
    escapement! [5] *(Sobbing.)* 'Twas my granpa gave it to
    me! *(He searches on the ground, Vladimir and Estragon
    likewise. Pozzo turns over with his foot the remains of
    Lucky's hat.)* Well now, isn't that just—

VLADIMIR. Perhaps it's in your fob. [6]

1. *totter* : walk unsteadily.
2. *reels* : walks even more unsteadily.
3. *sags* : bends, sinks down.
4. *half-hunter* : type of pocket-watch.
5. *deadbeat escapement* : an escapement is part of the mechanism of a
   watch, but 'deadbeat' means 'down and out' or 'exhausted',
   suggesting the watch is not working properly.
6. *fob* : a small watch pocket in the waistband of trousers.

POZZO. Wait! *(He doubles up* [1] *in an attempt to apply his ear to his stomach, listens. Silence.)* I hear nothing. *(He beckons* [2] *them to approach. Vladimir and Estragon go towards him, bend over his stomach.)* Surely one should hear the tick-tick.

VLADIMIR. Silence!

All listen, bent double.

ESTRAGON. I hear something.

POZZO. Where?

VLADIMIR. It's the heart.

POZZO *(disappointed)*. Damnation!

VLADIMIR. Silence!

ESTRAGON. Perhaps it has stopped.

They straighten up.

POZZO. Which of you smells so bad?

ESTRAGON. He has stinking breath and I have stinking feet.

POZZO. I must go.

ESTRAGON. And your half-hunter?

POZZO. I must have left it at the manor.

Silence.

ESTRAGON. Then adieu.

POZZO. Adieu.

VLADIMIR. Adieu.

POZZO. Adieu.

Silence. No one moves.

---

1. *doubles up* : bends down low.
2. *beckons* : makes a sign to.

VLADIMIR. Adieu.

POZZO. Adieu.

ESTRAGON. Adieu.

Silence.

POZZO. And thank you.

VLADIMIR. Thank you.

POZZO. Not at all.

ESTRAGON. Yes yes.

POZZO. No no.

VLADIMIR. Yes yes.

ESTRAGON. No no.

Silence.

POZZO. I don't seem to be able... *(long hesitation)*... to depart.

ESTRAGON. Such is life.

> *Pozzo turns, moves away from Lucky towards the wings, paying out the rope [1] as he goes.*

VLADIMIR. You're going the wrong way.

POZZO. I need a running start. *(Having come to the end of the rope, i.e. off stage, he stops, turns, and cries.)* Stand back! *(Vladimir and Estragon stand back, look towards Pozzo. Crack of whip.)* On! On!

ESTRAGON. On!

VLADIMIR. On!

> *Lucky moves off.*

POZZO. Faster! *(He appears, crosses the stage preceded by Lucky. Vladimir and Estragon wave their hats. Exit Lucky.)* On!

---

1. *paying out the rope* : letting the rope go loose.

> On! *(On the point of disappearing in his turn he stops and
> turns. The rope tautens. Noise of Lucky falling off.)* Stool!
> *(Vladimir fetches stool and gives it to Pozzo, who throws it
> to Lucky.)* Adieu!

VLADIMIR. ESTRAGON. *(waving)* Adieu! Adieu!

POZZO. Up! Pig! *(Noise of Lucky getting up.)* On! *(Exit Pozzo.)*
Faster! On! Adieu! Pig! Yip! Adieu!

Long silence.

VLADIMIR. That passed the time.

ESTRAGON. It would have passed in any case.

VLADIMIR. Yes, but not so rapidly.

ESTRAGON. What do we do now?

VLADIMIR. I don't know.

ESTRAGON. Let's go.

VLADIMIR. We can't.

ESTRAGON. Why not?

VLADIMIR. We're waiting for Godot.

ESTRAGON *(despairingly).* Ah!

VLADIMIR. How they've changed!

ESTRAGON. Who?

VLADIMIR. Those two.

ESTRAGON. That's the idea, let's make a little conversation.

VLADIMIR. Haven't they?

ESTRAGON. What?

VLADIMIR. Changed.

ESTRAGON. Very likely. [1] They all change. Only we can't.

VLADIMIR. Likely! It's certain. Didn't you see them?

---

1. *likely* : probably.

ESTRAGON. I suppose I did. But I don't know them.

VLADIMIR. Yes you do know them.

ESTRAGON. No I don't know them.

VLADIMIR. We know them, I tell you. You forget everything.
         (Pause. To himself.) Unless they're not the same…

ESTRAGON. Why didn't they recognize us then?

VLADIMIR. That means nothing. I too pretended not to recognize
         them. And then nobody ever recognizes us.

ESTRAGON. Forget it. What we need—Ow! *(Vladimir does not
         react.)* Ow!

VLADIMIR *(to himself)*. Unless they're not the same…

ESTRAGON. Didi! It's the other foot!

         He goes hobbling towards the mound.

VLADIMIR. Unless they're not the same…

BOY *(off)*. Mister!

         Estragon halts. Both look towards the voice.

ESTRAGON. Off we go again.

VLADIMIR. Approach, my child.

         Enter Boy, timidly. He halts.

BOY. Mister Albert…?[1]

VLADIMIR. Yes.

ESTRAGON. What do you want?

VLADIMIR. Approach.

         The Boy does not move.

1. *Mr Albert…?* : Paul-Louis Mignon (*L'Avant Scène*, June, 1964, p. 8)
    says that Beckett told him the dialogue between Vladimir and
    the boy was based on that between the Glazier and his son in the
    play *Eleuthéria*, which Beckett had written before *Godot*, though
    it was not published until later.

ESTRAGON *(forcibly)*. Approach when you're told, can't you?

> *The Boy advances timidly, halts.*

VLADIMIR. What is it?

BOY. Mr. Godot…

VLADIMIR. Obviously… *(Pause.)* Approach.

ESTRAGON *(violently)*. Will you approach! *(The Boy advances timidly.)* What kept you so late?

VLADIMIR. You have a message from Mr. Godot?

BOY. Yes, sir.

VLADIMIR. Well, what is it?

ESTRAGON. What kept you so late?

> *The Boy looks at them in turn, not knowing to which he should reply.*

VLADIMIR *(to Estragon)*. Let him alone.

ESTRAGON *(violently)*. You let me alone! *(Advancing, to the Boy.)* Do you know what time it is?

BOY *(recoiling)*. It's not my fault, sir.

ESTRAGON. And whose is it? Mine?

BOY. I was afraid, sir.

ESTRAGON. Afraid of what? Of us? *(Pause.)* Answer me!

VLADIMIR. I know what it is, he was afraid of the others.

ESTRAGON. How long have you been here?

BOY. A good while, sir.

VLADIMIR. You were afraid of the whip.

BOY. Yes, sir.

VLADIMIR. The roars.

BOY. Yes, sir.

VLADIMIR. The two big men.

BOY. Yes, sir.

VLADIMIR. Do you know them?

BOY. No, sir.

VLADIMIR. Are you a native of these parts? *(Silence.)* Do you belong to these parts?

BOY. Yes, sir.

ESTRAGON. That's all a pack of lies. *(Shaking the Boy by the arm.)* Tell us the truth.

BOY *(trembling).* But it is the truth, sir!

VLADIMIR. Will you let him alone! What's the matter with you? *(Estragon releases the Boy, moves away, covering his face with his hands. Vladimir and the Boy observe him. Estragon drops his hands. His face is convulsed.)* What's the matter with you?

ESTRAGON. I'm unhappy.

VLADIMIR. Not really! Since when?

ESTRAGON. I'd forgotten.

VLADIMIR. Extraordinary the tricks that memory plays! *(Estragon tries to speak, renounces, limps to his place, sits down and begins to take off his boots. To Boy.)* Well?

BOY. Mr. Godot—

VLADIMIR. I've seen you before, haven't I?

BOY. I don't know, sir.

VLADIMIR. You don't know me?

BOY. No, sir.

VLADIMIR. It wasn't you came yesterday?

BOY. No, sir.

VLADIMIR. This is your first time?

BOY. Yes, sir.

> *Silence.*

VLADIMIR. Words, words. *(Pause.)* Speak.

BOY *(in a rush)*. Mr. Godot told me to tell you he won't come this
    evening but surely tomorrow.

    Silence.

VLADIMIR. Is that all?

BOY. Yes, sir.

    Silence.

VLADIMIR. You work for Mr. Godot?

BOY. Yes, sir.

VLADIMIR. What do you do?

BOY. I mind the goats, sir.

VLADIMIR. Is he good to you?

BOY. Yes, sir.

VLADIMIR. He doesn't beat you?

BOY. No, sir, not me.

VLADIMIR. Whom does he beat?

BOY. He beats my brother, sir.

VLADIMIR. Ah, you have a brother?

BOY. Yes, sir.

VLADIMIR. What does he do?

BOY. He minds the sheep, sir. [1]

VLADIMIR. And why doesn't he beat you?

BOY. I don't know, sir.

VLADIMIR. He must be fond of you.

BOY. I don't know, sir.

    Silence.

---

1. *He minds the sheep, sir* : possibly a reference to Abel: 'And Abel
   was a keeper of sheep'(Genesis 4:2).

VLADIMIR. Does he give you enough to eat? *(The Boy hesitates.)* Does he feed you well?

BOY. Fairly well, sir.

VLADIMIR. You're not unhappy? *(The Boy hesitates.)* Do you hear me?

BOY. Yes, sir.

VLADIMIR. Well?

BOY. I don't know, sir.

VLADIMIR. You don't know if you're unhappy or not?

BOY. No, sir.

VLADIMIR. You're as bad as myself. *(Silence.)* Where do you sleep?

BOY. In the loft, sir.

VLADIMIR. With your brother?

BOY. Yes, sir.

VLADIMIR. In the hay?

BOY. Yes, sir.

   Silence.

VLADIMIR. All right, you may go.

BOY. What am I to say to Mr. Godot, sir?

VLADIMIR. Tell him... *(he hesitates)*... tell him you saw us. *(Pause.)* You did see us, didn't you?

BOY. Yes, sir.

   He steps back, hesitates, turns and exit running. The light suddenly fails. In a moment it is night. The moon rises at back, mounts in the sky, stands still, shedding [1] a pale light on the scene.

---

   1. *shedding* : letting fall.

VLADIMIR. At last! *(Estragon gets up and goes towards Vladimir, a boot in each hand. He puts them down at the edge of stage, straightens and contemplates the moon.)* What are you doing?

ESTRAGON. Pale for weariness. [1]

VLADIMIR. Eh?

ESTRAGON. Of climbing heaven and gazing on the likes of us.

VLADIMIR. Your boots. What are you doing with your boots?

ESTRAGON *(turning to look at the boots)*. I'm leaving them there. *(Pause.)* Another will come, [2] just as... as... as me, but with smaller feet, and they'll make him happy.

VLADIMIR. But you can't go barefoot!

ESTRAGON. Christ did.

VLADIMIR. Christ! What's Christ got to do with it? You're not going to compare yourself to Christ!

ESTRAGON. All my life I've compared myself to him.

VLADIMIR. But where he lived it was warm, it was dry!

ESTRAGON. Yes. And they crucified quick.

Silence.

VLADIMIR. We've nothing more to do here.

ESTRAGON. Nor anywhere else.

1. *Pale for weariness . . . Of climbing heaven and gazing on the likes of us :* from the first lines of Shelley's 'To the Moon': 'Art thou pale for weariness/Of climbing heaven and gazing on the earth...'

2. *Another will come :* a reference to the words of John the Baptist in *Mark, Luke* and *John,* where (in the version in *Mark*) he says: 'There cometh one mightier than I after me, the latchet of whose shoes I am not worthy to stoop down and loose.' The idea is converted into comedy when Estragon takes up the Biblical reference to Christ's shoes and bathetically transforms it into the idea that the other who follows will have smaller feet. This leads on to Estragon's comparing himself to Christ.

VLADIMIR. Ah Gogo, don't go on like that. Tomorrow everything will be better.

ESTRAGON. How do you make that out?

VLADIMIR. Did you not hear what the child said?

ESTRAGON. No.

VLADIMIR. He said that Godot was sure to come tomorrow. *(Pause.)* What do you say to that?

ESTRAGON. Then all we have to do is to wait on here.

VLADIMIR. Are you mad? We must take cover. *(He takes Estragon by the arm.)* Come on.

He draws Estragon after him. Estragon yields, then resists. They halt.

ESTRAGON *(looking at the tree).* Pity we haven't got a bit of rope.

VLADIMIR. Come on. It's cold.

He draws Estragon after him. As before.

ESTRAGON. Remind me to bring a bit of rope tomorrow.

VLADIMIR. Yes. Come on.

He draws him after him. As before.

ESTRAGON. How long have we been together all the time now?

VLADIMIR. I don't know. Fifty years perhaps.

ESTRAGON. Do you remember the day I threw myself into the Rhone?

VLADIMIR. We were grape-harvesting.

ESTRAGON. You fished me out.

VLADIMIR. That's all dead and buried.

ESTRAGON. My clothes dried in the sun.

VLADIMIR. There's no good harking back on that.[1] Come on.

1. *harking back on that* : remembering that nostalgically.

He draws him after him. As before.

ESTRAGON. Wait.

VLADIMIR. I'm cold!

ESTRAGON. Wait! *(He moves away from Vladimir.)* I wonder if we
wouldn't have been better off alone, each one for
himself. *(He crosses the stage and sits down on the
mound.)* We weren't made for the same road.

VLADIMIR *(without anger)*. It's not certain.

ESTRAGON. No, nothing is certain.

*Vladimir slowly crosses the stage and sits down beside
Estragon.*

VLADIMIR. We can still part, if you think it would be better.

ESTRAGON. It's not worth while now.

Silence.

VLADIMIR. No, it's not worth while now.

Silence.

ESTRAGON. Well, shall we go?

VLADIMIR. Yes, let's go.

They do not move.

CURTAIN

ACTIVITIES

Comprehension Questions

Pages 5-8,
to 'This is getting alarming.'

1. What is Estragon referring to when he says, 'Nothing to be done'?

2. What different meaning does Vladimir give to those first words of Estragon?

3. Why does Vladimir address Estragon as if he were royalty? (p. 6)

4. Why is Estragon's reply to Vladimir's question about where he spent the night surprising? (p. 6)

5. What suggestions are there already on the first three pages of

   a) uncertainty;

   b) pessimism?
   Are there any suggestions of optimism?

6. What two different complaints are the two men suffering from?

7. On p. 7, how does Vladimir again give a more serious significance to a mundane remark of Estragon?

8. 'Sometimes I feel it coming all the same.' What does the 'it' in Vladimir's remark refer to?

9. What makes Vladimir's repetition of Estragon's opening expostulation ('Nothing to be done') ironical? (p. 8)

10. Can you think what might be the significance of Vladimir's constant 'business' with his hat? (p. 8)

11. Vladimir says: 'This is getting alarming.' What might be getting alarming?

12. Look at the stage directions in this section of the text. Find words which suggest a) the physical and b) the emotional state of the characters. Complete the grid.

	VLADIMIR	**ESTRAGON**
Words suggesting the physical state of the characters		
Words suggesting the emotional state of the characters		

13. Write a summary of this section.

A C T I V I T I E S

Pages 8-11:
Silence . . . Estragon: 'People are bloody ignorant apes.'

1. How does Vladimir show optimism at this point? (p. 8)

2. Why does Vladimir break into a hearty laugh, then stifle the laugh? (p. 9)

3. What is the effect of the frequent repetition of 'nothing' in these opening pages?

4. Why is Estragon irritable with Vladimir? (p. 9)

5. Do you find it surprising when Estragon tells us he was a poet. Why?/Why not?

6. How is the tone of the dialogue deepened at this point (pp. 10-11)?

7. ESTRAGON: I'm going.

   He does not move.

   Comment on this contrast between action and expression of intention here.

8. On p. 10, how does Beckett draw the audience's attention to the theatrical nature of what it is watching?

9. Describe the content of the dialogue about the two thieves and the way in which it is conducted.

10. ESTRAGON: People are bloody ignorant apes.

    What is the effect of Estragon's concluding remark in this dialogue?

11. Look at the stage directions in this section of the text. Find words which suggest a) the physical and b) the emotional state of the characters. Complete the grid.

	VLADIMIR	**ESTRAGON**
Words suggesting the physical state of the characters		
Words suggesting the emotional state of the characters		

12. Summarise this section.

ACTIVITIES

Pages 11-14:
He rises painfully . . . Vladimir (feebly): 'All right.'

1. Why does Vladimir drop Estragon's boot hastily and say 'Pah!'

2. Vladimir mentions for the first time the reason why they can't go: 'We're waiting for Godot.' (p. 12) What might be the reaction of someone seeing the play for the first time to this first reference to Godot?

3. Vladimir tells Estragon angrily: 'Nothing is certain when you're about.' Find words and expressions which contribute to the idea of uncertainty in the dialogue on pp. 12-14. What kinds of uncertainty are suggested, e.g. about place? Complete the grid.

WORDS AND EXPRESSIONS OF UNCERTAINTY	KIND OF UNCERTAINTY

4.   Why does Vladimir accuse Estragon of being merciless? (p. 13)

5.   How do you think an actor should deliver Vladimir's question 'What'll we do?' (p. 14)

6.   Look at the stage directions in this section (but include the whole of p. 14). Find words which suggest the physical and the emotional state of the characters. Complete the grid.

	VLADIMIR	ESTRAGON
Words suggesting the physical state of the characters		
Words suggesting the emotional state of the characters		

7.   Look at the three grids showing words suggesting Vladimir and Estragon's physical and emotional states. Can we discern any difference(s) between the two men? If so, what difference(s)?

8.   Summarise this section.

ACTIVITIES

Pages 14-16:
Estragon sits down on the mound . . . Vladimir: 'It's for the kidneys.'

1. What is the horror of his situation to which Estragon is restored? (p. 14)

2. Why does Vladimir insist that Estragon should not tell him his dream? (p. 15)

3. What would 'be too bad, really too bad'? (p. 15)

4. What do you imagine Estragon really thinks of 'the beauty of the way' and 'the goodness of the wayfarers'? (p. 15)

5. Why does Vladimir tell Estragon so vehemently to stop telling his joke? (p. 16)

6. How and why is a tender moment destroyed on p. 16?

7. Which of the two characters manipulates the other in this section of the text?

8. Note the stage directions in this section. What do they tell us about each of the characters? Complete the grid.

STAGE DIRECTION	WHAT IT SUGGESTS ABOUT THE CHARACTER

ACTIVITIES

STAGE DIRECTION	WHAT IT SUGGESTS ABOUT THE CHARACTER

9. Summarise this section.

ACTIVITIES

Pages 16-20:
(Silence. *Estragon looks attentively at the tree*) . . . Vladimir (distinctly).
'We got rid of them.'

1. How serious are Vladimir and Estragon about hanging themselves? (pp. 16-18)

2. How are their vagueness and uncertainty about their expectations of Godot conveyed?

3. How is their desperate situation suggested?

4. Vladimir says: 'You'd make me laugh, if it wasn't prohibited.' In what two senses may laughter be prohibited to him? (p. 20)

5. Summarise this section.

Pages 20-3:
Silence. They remain motionless . . . Estragon: ' Like to finish it?'

1. How is their physical and emotional state conveyed at the beginning of this section of the text?

2. What signs do they show of panic? (p. 20)

3. What phrase on p. 20 suggests the insubstantiality of Godot?

4. What part does silence play in the theatrical effect of the play at this point?

5. How is the uncertainty of their situation further developed in this section of the text?

6. Which of the two shows the greater optimism in these pages?

7.   Why is the repetition of 'Nothing to be done' so effective on p. 23?

8.   Summarise this section.

Pages 23-7:
A terrible cry, close at hand . . . He drinks from the bottle, puts it down and begins to eat.

1.   What are the reactions of Vladimir and Estragon to the terrible cry? What three words, by describing their physical behaviour, indicate their state of mind immediately before the entry of Pozzo and Lucky? (p. 23)

2.   What are the reactions of Vladimir and Estragon when they hear Lucky falling? (p. 23)

3.   What does Estragon wonder about Pozzo? (p. 24)

4.   'Made in God's image': In your option is Pozzo suggesting that he, Vladimir and Estragon have something in common in that all three are made in God's image or that he himself is God and that the two tramps are made in his image?

5.   How does this passage (pp. 24-5) increase the uncertainty about the identity of Godot?

6.   What seems to be the relationship between Pozzo and Lucky?

7.   What adjectives and adverbs are used to describe Pozzo in this section of the text? What impression do they give of him?

ACTIVITIES

8. Pozzo says, 'I cannot go for long without the society of my likes.' How is this reference to his 'likes' made ironic in the context?

9. Describe Pozzo's way of speaking a) to Vladimir and Estragon; b) to Lucky.

10. What contrasts are made between Pozzo and the two tramps in this sequence?

11. Summarise this section.

Pages 27-31:
Silence . . . He puffs at his pipe.

1. Vladimir and Estragon's attention now turns to Lucky. What do they note about him? (pp. 28-9)

2. How are certainty and uncertainty suggested in this passage where the two tramps focus their attention on Lucky?

3. Pozzo tells Vladimir and Estragon to leave Lucky in peace. What is ironic about this? (p. 29)

4. How does Pozzo show his self-indulgence and self-satisfaction, his insensitivity to Lucky and his condescension to Estragon? (pp. 29-30)

5. Contrast the way Lucky is addressed by Estragon and the way Pozzo speaks to him. What is Pozzo's reaction to the way Estragon addresses Lucky?

6. Summarise this section.

Pages 31-6:
Vladimir (exploding): 'It's a scandal!' . . . Lucky weeps.

1. What is Vladimir scandalised by? Does Estragon agree with him?

2. How far do you feel Pozzo is sincere in his politeness to the tramps after they have protested at his treatment of Lucky?

3. How does Pozzo show his self-indulgence on pp. 31-2?

4. What indication does Pozzo give on p. 32 that he does not wish to show any weakness?

5. What are the different reactions of Vladimir and Estragon to Pozzo on p. 32?

6. What argument does Pozzo use to persuade Vladimir not to leave? (pp. 32-3)

7. 'If this goes on much longer we'll soon be old friends.' In what way is Pozzo's remark ironic? (p. 33)

8. Why does Pozzo not want the question of why Lucky doesn't put down his bags to get lost? (p. 34)

9. Why does Beckett give to Pozzo the stage business with the vaporizer? (p. 34)

10. What do you think is implied when Pozzo says 'I might just as well have been in his shoes and he in mine'? (p. 36)

11. Pozzo usually speaks formally, even pompously. On p. 36, what expression contrasts with Pozzo's general style of speech and what is the effect of this contrast?

12. Summarise this section.

A C T I V I T I E S

Pages 36-40:
Estragon: ' He's crying' . . . Pozzo: 'What have I done with my pipe?'

1. Why do you think Pozzo encourages Estragon to comfort Lucky? (p. 37)

2. Why do you think Pozzo says it's a good sign that Estragon's leg is bleeding? (p. 37)

3. VLADIMIR: *(tenderly)*. I'll carry you. *(Pause)*. If necessary.
    What is comical about this? (p. 43)

4. What is suggested by Pozzo's remark: 'The tears of the world are a constant quantity'? (p. 37) What does he then imply by: 'It is true the population has increased.'

5. How does Estragon show his feelings about Lucky after being kicked by him?

6. In this section of the text what changes take place in Vladimir and Estragon's feelings towards Pozzo and Lucky?

7. Trace the changing feelings of Pozzo during these pages. How sincere is he?

8. Summarise this section.

Pages 40-4:
Vladimir: 'Charming evening we're having' . . . Long silence
(end of Pozzo's long speech)

1. In the dialogue on p. 40 (to Vladimir's exit) what are their various comments on the nature of the action we are observing? What is the dramatic function of these remarks?

2. The setting of the play is 'A road. A tree.' When Vladimir hastens towards the wings, Estragon tells him 'End of the corridor, on the left', what is the theatrical effect of his remark? (p. 40)

3. Estragon says, 'It's all over.' What is all over? (p. 41)

4. What treat did Vladimir miss? (p. 41)

5. Study the stage directions regarding Vladimir on p. 41 and then describe what you imagine he is feeling.

6. On p. 42 how is the idea of waiting emphasised?

7. On these pages how is the difficulty of human action suggested?

8. What might be the significance of Estragon's giving his name as Adam? (p. 43)

9. Can you think of any reason why Pozzo doesn't listen when Estragon gives his name as Adam?

10. What is the main point Pozzo is making in his speech?

11. Look at the stage directions in Pozzo's speech.

   a) Why does Beckett prescribe frequent shifts between the lyrical and the prosaic in Pozzo's manner of delivery of his lines?

   b) What are the reactions of the three other characters during the speech?

   c) Describe Pozzo's gestures during his speech.

   d) What adjectives would you use to describe Pozzo's way of speaking during this scene?

12. Summarise this section.

ACTIVITIES

Pages 44-9:
Estragon: 'So long as one knows' ... *Pozzo: 'True!'*

1. In the brief dialogue between Vladimir and Estragon the idea of waiting is again referred to. What seems to be their attitude to the waiting?

2. Pozzo and the two tramps discuss his speech as a theatrical performance, even raising the question of whether it was tedious. Why does Beckett have them do this? (pp. 44-5)

3. During the silence in the middle of p. 45 Pozzo, the stage direction tells us, 'struggles inwardly'. Why do you think he is doing so?

4. Beckett saw Lucky's dance as a metaphor for human existence. What view of human existence does his dance imply? (p. 47)

5. Comment on the names suggested for Lucky's dance by Vladimir and Estragon.

6. Lucky's name for the dance is The Net. What is the significance of this?

7. What seems to be the reason why Pozzo, Vladimir and Estragon take off their hats? (p. 48)

8. What is ironic about Pozzo's comment, 'Stoutly reasoned!' (p. 49)

9. Summarise this section.

ACTIVITIES

Pages 49-55:
Silence. They put on their hats ... Vladimir examines the hat, peers inside it.

1. Pozzo says Lucky can't think without his hat. What is the ironic contrast between Lucky and the other three characters? (p. 49)

2. How is the distance between intention and action again indicated in this scene? (pp. 49-50)

3. What do the stage directions reveal of the reactions of the other three characters to Lucky's speech? (p. 50)

4. Try to outline the main argument (if you can find one) of Lucky's speech. (pp. 51-5).

5. Is there any similarity between the situation of Lucky and that of the two tramps?

6. What is the function of the allusions to Shakespeare, Verlaine and others in Lucky's speech?

7. Why does Beckett make Lucky refer to non-existent 'authorities' and why are there so many vulgar references in his speech?

8. How is Lucky finally silenced?

ACTIVITIES

Pages 55-9:
Pozzo: 'Give me that!' . . . Long silence.

1. Comment on the contrast between Pozzo's treatment of Lucky and his behaviour towards Vladimir and Estragon. (pp. 55-6)

2. What verbs suggest the feeble state of Lucky? (p. 56)

3. By p.59 how many objects has Pozzo lost? What significance, if any, can we attach to these losses?

4. Why does Beckett make the farewell of Pozzo into an elaborate comic routine? (p. 57)

5. Silences play a very important part in the play, as do moments of motionlessness. Comment on the silences and motionless moments on pp. 57-9.

6. Summarise this section.

Pages 57-64:
Vladimir: 'That passed the time' . . . turns and exit running.

1. How are the themes of waiting, uncertainty, time and memory kept before us in the scene leading to the entry of the boy?

2. How are we given the impression that this scene with the boy has happened before?

3. How is the theme of uncertainty continued in the scene with the boy? Find words or expressions which suggest different kinds of uncertainty – uncertainties of time, place, memory, event, identity, behaviour. Complete the grid.

A C T I V I T I E S

WORDS AND EXPRESSIONS	KIND OF UNCERTAINTY

4. Summarise this section.

ACTIVITIES

Pages 64-7:
The light suddenly fails . . . to the end of the act.

1. How does Estragon deflate the romanticism of the quotation from Shelley? (p. 65)

2. What is Estragon implying when he says that where Christ lived they crucified quick? (p. 65)

3. Which character seems more optimistic in this scene? Check your impression by completing the grid.

OPTIMISTIC EXPRESSIONS	PESSIMISTIC EXPRESSIONS	CHARACTER SPEAKING

4. Why does the end of the act leave us with a sense of uncertainty and stasis?

5. Summarise this section.

Act II

Next day. Same time. Same place.

Estragon's boots front centre, heels together, toes splayed. [1]
Lucky's hat at same place.

The tree has four or five leaves.

Enter Vladimir agitatedly. He halts and looks long at the tree, then suddenly begins to move feverishly about the stage. He halts before the boots, picks one up, examines it, sniffs [2] it, manifests disgust, puts it back carefully. Comes and goes. Halts extreme right and gazes into distance off, shading his eyes with his hand. Comes and goes. Halts extreme left, as before. Comes and goes. Halts suddenly and begins to sing loudly.

VLADIMIR. A dog came in—[3]

Having begun too high he stops, clears his throat, resumes.

> A dog came in the kitchen
> And stole a crust of bread.

1. *splayed* : pointing outwards.
2. *sniffs* : smells.
3. *A dog came in* . . . : Beckett's translation of a popular German round-song, the form of which is cyclical, and therefore appropriate to the cyclical action of Beckett's play.

Then cook up with a ladle [1]
And beat him till he was dead.

Then all the dogs came running
And dug the dog a tomb—

He stops, broods, [2] resumes:

Then all the dogs came running
And dug the dog a tomb
And wrote upon the tombstone
For the eyes of dogs to come:

A dog came in the kitchen
And stole a crust of bread.
Then cook up with a ladle
And beat him till he was dead.

Then all the dogs came running
And dug the dog a tomb—

He stops, broods, resumes:

Then all the dogs came running
And dug the dog a tomb—

He stops, broods. Softly.

And dug the dog a tomb...

He remains a moment silent and motionless, then begins to move feverishly about the stage. He halts before the tree, comes and goes, before the boots, comes and goes, halts extreme right, gazes into distance, extreme left, gazes into distance. Enter Estragon right, barefoot, head bowed. He slowly crosses the stage. Vladimir turns and sees him.

1. *ladle* : kitchen utensil, a type of large spoon for serving soup, for example.
2. *broods* : thinks.

VLADIMIR. You again! *(Estragon halts, but does not raise his head. Vladimir goes towards him.)* Come here till I embrace you.

ESTRAGON. Don't touch me!

Vladimir holds back, pained.

VLADIMIR. Do you want me to go away? *(Pause.)* Gogo! *(Pause. Vladimir observes him attentively.)* Did they beat you? *(Pause.)* Gogo! *(Estragon remains silent, head bowed.)* Where did you spend the night?

ESTRAGON. Don't touch me! Don't question me! Don't speak to me! Stay with me!

VLADIMIR. Did I ever leave you? You let me go. Look at me. *(Estragon does not raise his head. Violently.)* Will you look at me!

Estragon raises his head. They look long at each other, then suddenly embrace, clapping each other on the back. End of the embrace. Estragon, no longer supported, almost falls.

ESTRAGON. What a day!

VLADIMIR. Who beat you? Tell me.

ESTRAGON. Another day done with.

VLADIMIR. Not yet.

ESTRAGON. For me it's over and done with, no matter what happens. *(Silence.)* I heard you singing.

VLADIMIR. That's right, I remember.

ESTRAGON. That finished me. I said to myself, he's all alone, he thinks I'm gone for ever, and he sings.

VLADIMIR. One isn't master of one's moods. All day I've felt in great form. *(Pause.)* I didn't get up in the night, not once!

ESTRAGON *(sadly)*. You see, you piss better when I'm not there.

VLADIMIR. I missed you... and at the same time I was happy. Isn't that a queer thing?

ESTRAGON *(shocked).* Happy?

VLADIMIR. Perhaps it's not the right word.

ESTRAGON. And now?

VLADIMIR. Now?… *(Joyous.)* There you are again… *(Indifferent.)* There we are again… *(Gloomy.)* There I am again.

ESTRAGON. You see, you feel worse when I'm with you. I feel better alone, too.

VLADIMIR *(vexed).* [1] Then why do you always come crawling back?

ESTRAGON. I don't know.

VLADIMIR. No, but I do. It's because you don't know how to defend yourself. I wouldn't have let them beat you.

ESTRAGON. You couldn't have stopped them.

VLADIMIR. Why not?

ESTRAGON. There were ten of them.

VLADIMIR. No, I mean before they beat you. I would have stopped you from doing whatever it was you were doing.

ESTRAGON. I wasn't doing anything.

VLADIMIR. Then why did they beat you?

ESTRAGON. I don't know.

VLADIMIR. Ah no, Gogo, the truth is there are things escape you that don't escape me, you must feel it yourself.

ESTRAGON. I tell you I wasn't doing anything.

VLADIMIR. Perhaps you weren't. But it's the way of doing it that counts, the way of doing it, if you want to go on living.

ESTRAGON. I wasn't doing anything.

---

1. *vexed* : annoyed.

VLADIMIR. You must be happy, too, deep down, if you only knew it.

ESTRAGON. Happy about what?

VLADIMIR. To be back with me again.

ESTRAGON. Would you say so?

VLADIMIR. Say you are, even if it's not true.

ESTRAGON. What am I to say?

VLADIMIR. Say, I am happy.

ESTRAGON. I am happy.

VLADIMIR. So am I.

ESTRAGON. So am I.

VLADIMIR. We are happy.

ESTRAGON. We are happy. *(Silence.)* What do we do now, now that we are happy?

VLADIMIR. Wait for Godot. *(Estragon groans. Silence.)* Things have changed since yesterday.

ESTRAGON. And if he doesn't come?

VLADIMIR *(after a moment of bewilderment)*. We'll see when the time comes. *(Pause.)* I was saying that things have changed here since yesterday.

ESTRAGON. Everything oozes. [1]

VLADIMIR. Look at the tree.

ESTRAGON. It's never the same pus [2] from one second to the next.

VLADIMIR. The tree, look at the tree.

Estragon looks at the tree.

ESTRAGON. Was it not there yesterday?

1. *oozes* : flows out slowly.
2. *. . . the same pus . . .* : The reference is to the saw of Heraclitus, according to which we never bathe twice in the same stream.

VLADIMIR. Yes, of course it was there. Do you not remember? We nearly hanged ourselves from it. But you wouldn't. Do you not remember?

ESTRAGON. You dreamt it.

VLADIMIR. Is it possible that you've forgotten already?

ESTRAGON. That's the way I am. Either I forget immediately or I never forget.

VLADIMIR. And Pozzo and Lucky, have you forgotten them too?

ESTRAGON. Pozzo and Lucky?

VLADIMIR. He's forgotten everything!

ESTRAGON. I remember a lunatic who kicked the shins off me. Then he played the fool.

VLADIMIR. That was Lucky.

ESTRAGON. I remember that. But when was it?

VLADIMIR. And his keeper, do you not remember him?

ESTRAGON. He gave me a bone.

VLADIMIR. That was Pozzo.

ESTRAGON. And all that was yesterday, you say?

VLADIMIR. Yes, of course it was yesterday.

ESTRAGON. And here where we are now?

VLADIMIR. Where else do you think? Do you not recognize the place?

ESTRAGON *(suddenly furious)*. Recognize! What is there to recognize? All my lousy [1] life I've crawled about in the mud! And you talk to me about scenery! (Looking wildly about him.) Look at this muckheap! [2] I've never stirred from it!

VLADIMIR. Calm yourself, calm yourself.

---

1. *lousy* ['lauzi] : horrible (literally: infested with lice).
2. *muckheap* : pile of manure.

ESTRAGON. You and your landscapes! Tell me about the worms!

VLADIMIR. All the same, you can't tell me that this *(gesture)* bears any resemblance to... *(he hesitates)*... to the Macon country, for example. You can't deny there's a big difference.

ESTRAGON. The Macon country! Who's talking to you about the Macon country?

VLADIMIR. But you were there yourself, in the Macon country.

ESTRAGON. No, I was never in the Macon country. I've puked [1] my puke of a life away here, I tell you! Here! In the Cackon country! [2]

VLADIMIR. But we were there together, I could swear to it! Picking grapes for a man called... *(he snaps his fingers)*... can't think of the name of the man, at a place called... *(snaps his fingers)*... can't think of the name of the place, do you not remember?

ESTRAGON *(a little calmer)*. It's possible. I didn't notice anything.

VLADIMIR. But down there everything is red! [3]

ESTRAGON *(exasperated)*. I didn't notice anything, I tell you!

Silence. Vladimir sighs deeply.

VLADIMIR. You're a hard man to get on with, Gogo.

ESTRAGON. It'd be better if we parted.

1. *puked* : vomited (the noun 'puke' means 'vomit').
2. *In the Cackon country* : A pun based on caca, the word French and Italian children use for excrement. In South Wales, the forms 'cacka', 'cacky' and 'to cack on' can all be heard (see also p. 52, note). In the French version, Vladimir talks about the Vaucluse and Estragon says he has never been in the Vaucluse but has spent all his life here, in the Merdecluse. Beckett spent the latter part of the war years at Roussillon, in the *département* of the Vaucluse, in South-east France.
3. *But down there everything is red!* : An allusion to the red soil in the Roussillon area.

VLADIMIR. You always say that, and you always come crawling
          back.

ESTRAGON. The best thing would be to kill me, like the other.

VLADIMIR. What other? *(Pause.)* What other?

ESTRAGON. Like billions of others.

VLADIMIR *(sententious).* To every man his little cross. *(He sighs.)*
          Till he dies. *(Afterthought.)* And is forgotten.

ESTRAGON. In the meantime let us try and converse calmly, since
          we are incapable of keeping silent.

VLADIMIR. You're right, we're inexhaustible.

ESTRAGON. It's so we won't think.

VLADIMIR. We have that excuse.

ESTRAGON. It's so we won't hear

VLADIMIR. We have our reasons.

ESTRAGON. All the dead voices.

VLADIMIR. They make a noise like wings.

ESTRAGON. Like leaves. [1]

VLADIMIR. Like sand.

ESTRAGON. Like leaves.

    Silence.

VLADIMIR. They all speak together.

---

1. *Like leaves* : The dead voices, Estragon insists, make a noise like
    leaves. Given Beckett's knowledge of Dante, this seems to be an
    allusion to *Inferno* iii, 112-115. Fallen leaves are a traditional
    simile for the numberless dead, used by Homer (*Iliad* vi, l. 46),
    Virgil (*Aeneid* vi, 309-10) and Milton (*Paradise Lost*, l. 302-3), as
    well as by Dante. Cf. also *Isaiah*, xxxiv, 4: 'And all the host of
    heaven shall be dissolved, and the heavens shall be rolled
    together as a scroll: and all their host shall fall down, as the leaf
    falleth off from the tree, and as a falling fig from the fig tree.'
    Milton uses the simile to describe the fallen angels, now
    transformed into devils and damned to an eternity in hell.
    Estragon later says 'I'm in hell!' (p. 111)

ESTRAGON. Each one to itself.

Silence.

VLADIMIR. Rather they whisper.
ESTRAGON. They rustle. [1]
VLADIMIR. They murmur. [2]
ESTRAGON. They rustle.

Silence.

VLADIMIR. What do they say?
ESTRAGON. They talk about their lives.
VLADIMIR. To have lived is not enough for them.
ESTRAGON. They have to talk about it.
VLADIMIR. To be dead is not enough for them.
ESTRAGON. It is not sufficient.

Silence.

VLADIMIR. They make a noise like feathers.
ESTRAGON. Like leaves.
VLADIMIR. Like ashes.
ESTRAGON. Like leaves.

Long silence.

VLADIMIR. Say something!
ESTRAGON. I'm trying.

Long silence.

VLADIMIR *(in anguish).* Say anything at all!
ESTRAGON. What do we do now?

1. *rustle* ['rʌsəl] : make a dry light sound.
2. *murmur* ['məːmə] : make a low continuous indistinct sound.

VLADIMIR. Wait for Godot.

ESTRAGON. Ah!

Silence.

VLADIMIR. This is awful!

ESTRAGON. Sing something.

VLADIMIR. No no! *(He reflects.)* We could start all over again perhaps.

ESTRAGON. That should be easy.

VLADIMIR. It's the start that's difficult.

ESTRAGON. You can start from anything.

VLADIMIR. Yes, but you have to decide.

ESTRAGON. True.

Silence.

VLADIMIR. Help me!

ESTRAGON. I'm trying.

Silence.

VLADIMIR. When you seek you hear.

ESTRAGON. You do.

VLADIMIR. That prevents you from finding.

ESTRAGON. It does.

VLADIMIR. That prevents you from thinking.

ESTRAGON. You think all the same.

VLADIMIR. No, no, impossible.

ESTRAGON. That's the idea, let's contradict each other.

VLADIMIR. Impossible.

ESTRAGON. You think so?

VLADIMIR. We're in no danger of ever thinking any more.

ESTRAGON. Then what are we complaining about?

VLADIMIR. Thinking is not the worst.

ESTRAGON. Perhaps not. But at least there's that.

VLADIMIR. That what?

ESTRAGON. That's the idea, let's ask each other questions.

VLADIMIR. What do you mean, at least there's that?

ESTRAGON. That much less misery.

VLADIMIR. True.

ESTRAGON. Well? If we gave thanks for our mercies?

VLADIMIR. What is terrible is to have thought.

ESTRAGON. But did that ever happen to us?

VLADIMIR. Where are all these corpses from?

ESTRAGON. These skeletons.

VLADIMIR. Tell me that.

ESTRAGON. True.

VLADIMIR. We must have thought a little.

ESTRAGON. At the very beginning.

VLADIMIR. A charnel-house![1] A charnel-house!

ESTRAGON. You don't have to look.

VLADIMIR. You can't help looking.

ESTRAGON. True.

VLADIMIR. Try as one may.

ESTRAGON. I beg your pardon?

VLADIMIR. Try as one may.

ESTRAGON. We should turn resolutely towards Nature.

VLADIMIR. We've tried that.

ESTRAGON. True.

VLADIMIR. Oh, it's not the worst, I know.

1. *charnel* ['tʃɑːnəl] *-house* : place for keeping dead human bodies or bones.

ESTRAGON. What?

VLADIMIR. To have thought.

ESTRAGON. Obviously.

VLADIMIR. But we could have done without it.

ESTRAGON. Que voulez-vous?

VLADIMIR. I beg your pardon?

ESTRAGON. Que voulez-vous?

VLADIMIR. Ah! que voulez-vous. Exactly.

Silence.

ESTRAGON. That wasn't such a bad little canter. [1]

VLADIMIR. Yes, but now we'll have to find something else.

ESTRAGON. Let me see.

He takes off his hat, concentrates.

VLADIMIR. Let me see. (*He takes off his hat, concentrates. Long silence.*) Ah!

They put on their hats, relax.

ESTRAGON. Well?

VLADIMIR. What was I saying, we could go on from there.

ESTRAGON. What were you saying when?

VLADIMIR. At the very beginning.

ESTRAGON. The beginning of WHAT?

VLADIMIR. This evening… I was saying… I was saying… I'm not a historian. Wait… we embraced… we were happy… happy… what do we do now that we're happy… go on waiting… waiting… let me think… it's coming… go on waiting… now that we're happy… let me see… ah! The tree!

1. *canter* : gentle gallop.

ESTRAGON. The tree?

VLADIMIR. Do you not remember?

ESTRAGON. I'm tired.

VLADIMIR. Look at it.

> *They look at the tree.*

ESTRAGON. I see nothing.

VLADIMIR. But yesterday evening it was all black and bare. And now it's covered with leaves.

ESTRAGON. Leaves?

VLADIMIR. In a single night.

ESTRAGON. It must be the Spring.

VLADIMIR. But in a single night!

ESTRAGON. I tell you we weren't here yesterday. Another of your nightmares.

VLADIMIR. And where were we yesterday evening according to you?

ESTRAGON. How do I know? In another compartment. There's no lack of void.

VLADIMIR *(sure of himself)*. Good. We weren't here yesterday evening. Now what did we do yesterday evening?

ESTRAGON. Do?

VLADIMIR. Try and remember.

ESTRAGON. Do... I suppose we blathered.

VLADIMIR *(controlling himself)*. About what?

ESTRAGON. Oh... this and that, I suppose, nothing in particular. *(With assurance.)* Yes, now I remember, yesterday evening we spent blathering about nothing in particular. That's been going on now for half a century.

VLADIMIR. You don't remember any fact, any circumstance?

ESTRAGON *(weary)*. Don't torment me, Didi.

VLADIMIR. The sun, The moon. Do you not remember?

ESTRAGON. They must have been there, as usual.

VLADIMIR. You didn't notice anything out of the ordinary?

ESTRAGON. Alas!

VLADIMIR. And Pozzo? And Lucky?

ESTRAGON. Pozzo?

VLADIMIR. The bones.

ESTRAGON. They were like fishbones.

VLADIMIR. It was Pozzo gave them to you.

ESTRAGON. I don't know.

VLADIMIR. And the kick.

ESTRAGON. That's right, someone gave me a kick.

VLADIMIR. It was Lucky gave it to you.

ESTRAGON. And all that was yesterday?

VLADIMIR. Show your leg.

ESTRAGON. Which?

VLADIMIR. Both. Pull up your trousers. *(Estragon gives a leg to Vladimir, staggers.* [1] *Vladimir takes the leg. They stagger.)* Pull up your trousers.

ESTRAGON. I can't.

> *Vladimir pulls up the trousers, look at the leg, lets it go. Estragon almost falls.*

VLADIMIR. The other. *(Estragon gives the same leg.)* The other, pig! *(Estragon gives the other leg. Triumphantly.)* There's the wound! Beginning to fester! [2]

ESTRAGON. And what about it?

VLADIMIR *(letting go the leg)*. Where are your boots?

---

1. *staggers* : moves unsteadily as if about to fall.
2. *fester* : become infected and filled with pus.

ESTRAGON. I must have thrown them away.

VLADIMIR. When?

ESTRAGON. I don't know.

VLADIMIR. Why?

ESTRAGON *(exasperated).* I don't know why I don't know!

VLADIMIR. No, I mean why did you throw them away?

ESTRAGON *(exasperated).* Because they were hurting me!

VLADIMIR *(triumphantly, pointing at the boots).* There they are! *(Estragon looks at the boots.)* At the very spot where you left them yesterday!

Estragon goes towards the boots, inspects them closely.

ESTRAGON. They're not mine.

VLADIMIR *(stupified).* Not yours!

ESTRAGON. Mine were black. These are brown.

VLADIMIR. You're sure yours were black?

ESTRAGON. Well, they were a kind of grey.

VLADIMIR. And these are brown? Show.

ESTRAGON *(picking up a boot).* Well, they're a kind of green.

VLADIMIR. Show. *(Estragon hands him the boot. Vladimir inspects it, throws it down angrily.)* Well of all the—

ESTRAGON. You see, all that's a lot of bloody—

VLADIMIR. Ah! I see what it is. Yes, I see what's happened.

ESTRAGON. All that's a lot of bloody—

VLADIMIR. It's elementary. Someone came and took yours and left you his.

ESTRAGON. Why?

VLADIMIR. His were too tight for him, so he took yours.

ESTRAGON. But mine were too tight.

VLADIMIR. For you. Not for him.

ESTRAGON *(having tried in vain to work it out).* I'm tired! *(Pause.)* Let's go.

VLADIMIR. We can't.

ESTRAGON. Why not?

VLADIMIR. We're waiting for Godot.

ESTRAGON. Ah! *(Pause. Despairing.)* What'll we do, what'll we do!

VLADIMIR. There's nothing we can do.

ESTRAGON. But I can't go on like this!

VLADIMIR. Would you like a radish?

ESTRAGON. Is that all there is?

VLADIMIR. There are radishes and turnips.

ESTRAGON. Are there no carrots?

VLADIMIR. No. Anyway you overdo it with your carrots.

ESTRAGON. Then give me a radish. *(Vladimir fumbles in his pockets, finds nothing but turnips, finally brings out a radish and hands it to Estragon, who examines it, sniffs it.)* It's black!

VLADIMIR. It's a radish.

ESTRAGON. I only like the pink ones, you know that!

VLADIMIR. Then you don't want it?

ESTRAGON. I only like the pink ones!

VLADIMIR. Then give it back to me.

Estragon gives it back.

ESTRAGON. I'll go and get a carrot.

He does not move.

VLADIMIR. This is becoming really insignificant.

ESTRAGON. Not enough.

Silence.

VLADIMIR. What about trying them?

ESTRAGON. I've tried everything.

VLADIMIR. No, I mean the boots.

ESTRAGON. Would that be a good thing?

VLADIMIR. It'd pass the time. *(Estragon hesitates.)* I assure you, it'd be an occupation.

ESTRAGON. A relaxation.

VLADIMIR. A recreation.

ESTRAGON. A relaxation.

VLADIMIR. Try.

ESTRAGON. You'll help me?

VLADIMIR. I will of course.

ESTRAGON. We don't manage too badly, eh Didi, between the two of us?

VLADIMIR. Yes yes. Come on, we'll try the left first.

ESTRAGON. We always find something, eh Didi, to give us the impression we exist?

VLADIMIR *(impatiently)*. Yes yes, we're magicians. But let us persevere in what we have resolved, before we forget. *(He picks up a boot.)* Come on, give me your foot. *(Estragon raises his foot.)* The other, hog! *(Estragon raises the other foot.)* Higher! *(Wreathed together [1] they stagger about the stage. Vladimir succeeds finally in getting on the boot.)* Try and walk. *(Estragon walks.)* Well?

ESTRAGON. It fits.

VLADIMIR *(taking string from his pocket)*. We'll try and lace it.

ESTRAGON *(vehemently)*. No no, no laces, no laces!

VLADIMIR. You'll be sorry. Let's try the other. *(As before.)* Well?

ESTRAGON *(grudgingly)*. It fits too.

---

1. *Wreathed* [riːðd] *together* : Holding each other, entwined.

VLADIMIR. They don't hurt you?

ESTRAGON. Not yet.

VLADIMIR. Then you can keep them.

ESTRAGON. They're too big. [1]

VLADIMIR. Perhaps you'll have socks some day.

ESTRAGON. True.

VLADIMIR. Then you'll keep them?

ESTRAGON. That's enough about these boots.

VLADIMIR. Yes, but—

ESTRAGON *(violently)*. Enough! *(Silence.)* I suppose I might as well sit down.

He looks for a place to sit down, then goes and sits down on the mound.

VLADIMIR. That's where you were sitting yesterday evening.

ESTRAGON. If I could only sleep.

VLADIMIR. Yesterday you slept.

ESTRAGON. I'll try.

He resumes his foetal posture, his head between his knees.

VLADIMIR. Wait. *(He goes over and sits down beside Estragon and begins to sing in a loud voice.)*
Bye bye bye bye [2]
Bye bye—

ESTRAGON *(looking up angrily)*. Not so loud!

---

1. *They're too big* : Colin Duckworth tells us: 'Mr Beckett wrote me the following comment on this: 'The second day boots are no doubt same as first and Estragon's feet wasted, pined, shrunk and dwindled in interval. There's exegesis for you.' (See Duckworth's edition of *En attendant Godot*, p. 99.)

2. *Bye bye bye bye* : words used by mothers to encourage their babies to go to sleep.

VLADIMIR *(softly)*.

> Bye bye bye bye
> Bye bye bye bye
> Bye bye bye bye
> Bye bye...
> *(Estragon sleeps. Vladimir gets up softly, takes off his coat and lays it across Estragon's shoulders, then starts walking up and down, swinging his arms to keep himself warm. Estragon wakes with a start, jumps up, casts about wildly. Vladimir runs to him, puts his arms round him.)*
> There... there... Didi is there... don't be afraid...

ESTRAGON. Ah!

VLADIMIR. There... there... it's all over.

ESTRAGON. I was falling—

VLADIMIR. It's all over, it's all over.

ESTRAGON. I was on top of a—

VLADIMIR. Don't tell me! Come, we'll walk it off.

He takes Estragon by the arm and walks him up and down until Estragon refuses to go any further.

ESTRAGON. That's enough. I'm tired.

VLADIMIR. You'd rather be stuck there doing nothing?

ESTRAGON. Yes.

VLADIMIR. Please yourself.

He releases Estragon, picks up his coat and puts it on.

ESTRAGON. Let's go.

VLADIMIR. We can't.

ESTRAGON. Why not?

VLADIMIR. We're waiting for Godot.

ESTRAGON. Ah! *(Vladimir walks up and down.)* Can you not stay still?

VLADIMIR. I'm cold.

ESTRAGON. We came too soon.

VLADIMIR. It's always at nightfall.

ESTRAGON. But night doesn't fall.

VLADIMIR. It'll fall all of a sudden, like yesterday.

ESTRAGON. Then it'll be night.

VLADIMIR. And we can go.

ESTRAGON. Then it'll be day again. *(Pause. Despairing.)* What'll we do, what'll we do!

VLADIMIR *(halting, violently)*. Will you stop whining![1] I've had about my bellyful of your lamentations!

ESTRAGON. I'm going.

VLADIMIR *(seeing Lucky's hat)*. Well!

ESTRAGON. Farewell.

VLADIMIR. Lucky's hat. *(He goes towards it.)* I've been here an hour and never saw it. *(Very pleased.)* Fine!

ESTRAGON. You'll never see me again.

VLADIMIR. I knew it was the right place. Now our troubles are over. *(He picks up the hat, contemplates it, straightens it.)* Must have been a very fine hat. *(He puts it on in place of his own which he hands to Estragon.)* Here.

ESTRAGON. What?

VLADIMIR. Hold that.

> *Estragon takes Vladimir's hat.[2] Vladimir adjusts Lucky's hat on his head. Estragon puts on Vladimir's hat in place of his own which he hands to Vladimir. Vladimir takes Estragon's hat. Estragon adjusts Vladimir's hat on his head. Vladimir puts on Estragon's hat in place of Lucky's which he hands to*

---

1. *whining* [wʌɪnɪŋ] : complaining.
2. *Estragon takes Vladimir's hat* : A music-hall routine found both in the films of Laurel and Hardy and in the Marx Brothers' masterpiece, *Duck Soup* (1933).

Estragon. Estragon takes Lucky's hat. Vladimir adjusts Estragon's hat on his head. Estragon puts on Lucky's hat in place of Vladimir's which he hands to Vladimir. Vladimir takes his hat. Estragon adjusts Lucky's hat on his head. Vladimir puts on his hat in place of Estragon's which he hands to Estragon. Estragon takes his hat. Vladimir adjusts his hat on his head. Estragon puts on his hat in place of Lucky's which he hands to Vladimir. Vladimir takes Lucky's hat. Estragon adjusts his hat on his head. Vladimir puts on Lucky's hat in place of his own which he hands to Estragon. Estragon takes Vladimir's hat. Vladimir adjusts Lucky's hat on his head. Estragon hands Vladimir's hat back to Vladimir who takes it and hands it back to Estragon who takes it and hands it back to Vladimir who takes it and throws it down. How does it fit me?

ESTRAGON. How would I know?

VLADIMIR. No, but how do I look in it?

He turns his head coquettishly to and fro, minces [1] like a mannequin.

ESTRAGON. Hideous.

VLADIMIR. Yes, but not more so than usual?

ESTRAGON. Neither more nor less.

VLADIMIR. Then I can keep it. Mine irked [2] me. *(Pause.)* How shall I say? *(Pause.)* It itched me. [3]

He takes off Lucky's hat, peers into it, shakes it, knocks on the crown, puts it on again.

ESTRAGON. I'm going.

Silence.

1. *minces* [mɪnsəʒ] : moves in an effeminate way.
2. *irked* [əːkd] : annoyed.
3. *itched me* : irritated my skin.

VLADIMIR. Will you not play?

ESTRAGON. Play at what?

VLADIMIR. We could play at Pozzo and Lucky.

ESTRAGON. Never heard of it.

VLADIMIR. I'll do Lucky, you do Pozzo. (*He imitates Lucky sagging under the weight of his baggage. Estragon looks at him with stupefaction.*) Go on.

ESTRAGON. What am I to do?

VLADIMIR. Curse me!

ESTRAGON (*after reflection*). Naughty!

VLADIMIR. Stronger!

ESTRAGON. Gonococcus![1] Spirochaete![2]

Vladimir sways back and forth, doubled in two.

VLADIMIR. Tell me to think.

ESTRAGON. What?

VLADIMIR. Say, Think, pig!

ESTRAGON. Think, pig!

Silence.

VLADIMIR. I can't.

ESTRAGON. That's enough of that.

VLADIMIR. Tell me to dance.

ESTRAGON. I'm going.

VLADIMIR. Dance, hog! (*He writhes.[3] Exit Estragon left, precipitately.*) I can't! (*He looks up, misses Estragon.*) Gogo! (*He moves

---

1. *Gonococcus* : the micro-organism causing gonorrhoea.
2. *Spirochaete* : spiral-shaped bacterium causing syphilis.
3. *writhes* [rʌɪðz] : twists his body in a grotesque dancing movement.

wildly about the stage. Enter Estragon left, panting. He hastens towards Vladimir, falls into his arms.) There you are again at last!

ESTRAGON. I'm accursed!

VLADIMIR. Where were you! I thought you were gone for ever.

ESTRAGON. They're coming!

VLADIMIR. Who?

ESTRAGON. I don't know.

VLADIMIR. How many?

ESTRAGON. I don't know.

VLADIMIR *(triumphantly).* It's Godot! At last! Gogo! It's Godot! We're saved! Let's go and meet him! *(He drags Estragon towards the wings. Estragon resists, pulls himself free, exit right.)* Gogo! Come back! *(Vladimir runs to extreme left, scans* [1] *the horizon. Enter Estragon right, he hastens towards Vladimir, falls into his arms.)* There you are again!

ESTRAGON. I'm in hell!

VLADIMIR. Where were you?

ESTRAGON. They're coming there too!

VLADIMIR. We're surrounded! *(Estragon makes a rush towards back.)* Imbecile! There's no way out there. *(He takes Estragon by the arm and drags him towards front. Gesture towards front.)* There! Not a soul in sight! Off you go. Quick! *(He pushes Estragon towards auditorium. Estragon recoils in horror.)* You won't? *(He contemplates auditorium.)* Well, I can understand that. Wait till I see. *(He reflects.)* Your only hope left is to disappear.

ESTRAGON. Where?

---

1.   *scans* : looks along.

VLADIMIR. Behind the tree. *(Estragon hesitates.)* Quick! Behind the tree. *(Estragon goes and crouches*[1] *behind the tree, realizes he is not hidden, comes out from behind the tree.)* Decidedly this tree will not have been of the slightest use to us.

ESTRAGON *(calmer)*. I lost my head. Forgive me. It won't happen again. Tell me what to do.

VLADIMIR. There's nothing to do.

ESTRAGON. You go and stand there. *(He draws Vladimir to extreme right and places him with his back to the stage.)* There, don't move, and watch out. *(Vladimir scans horizon, screening*[2] *his eyes with his hand. Estragon runs and takes up same position, extreme left. They turn their heads and look at each other.)* Back to back like in the good old days! *(They continue to look at each other for a moment, then resume their watch. Long silence.)* Do you see anything coming?

VLADIMIR *(turning his head)*. What?

ESTRAGON *(louder)*. Do you see anything coming?

VLADIMIR. No.

ESTRAGON. Nor I.

They resume their watch. Silence.

VLADIMIR. You must have had a vision.

ESTRAGON *(turning his head)*. What?

VLADIMIR *(louder)*. You must have had a vision!

ESTRAGON. No need to shout!

They resume their watch. Silence.

---

1. *crouches* [kraʊtʃəz] : lowers his body by bending the knees, in order to hide.
2. *screening* : keeping the light from.

VLADIMIR
ESTRAGON } *(turning simultaneously).* Do you—

VLADIMIR. Oh, pardon!

ESTRAGON. Carry on.

VLADIMIR. No no, after you.

ESTRAGON. No no, you first.

VLADIMIR. I interrupted you.

ESTRAGON. On the contrary.

They glare[1] at each other angrily.

VLADIMIR. Ceremonious ape!

ESTRAGON. Punctilious pig!

VLADIMIR. Finish your phrase, I tell you!

ESTRAGON. Finish your own!

Silence. They draw closer, halt.

VLADIMIR. Moron!

ESTRAGON. That's the idea, let's abuse each other.

They turn, move apart, turn again and face each other.

VLADIMIR. Moron![2]

ESTRAGON. Vermin!

VLADIMIR. Abortion!

ESTRAGON. Morpion![3]

VLADIMIR. Sewer-rat![4]

ESTRAGON. Curate!

1. *glare* [glɛː] : look intensely.
2. *moron* ['mɔːrɒn] : idiot.
3. *morpion* : pubic louse (French word).
4. *sewer-rat* : rat that inhabits a sewer (underground pipe or passage that carries away waste matter to be purified).

VLADIMIR. Cretin!

ESTRAGON *(with finality)*. Crritic!

VLADIMIR. Oh!

He wilts, vanquished, and turns away.

ESTRAGON. Now let's make it up.

VLADIMIR. Gogo!

ESTRAGON. Didi!

VLADIMIR. Your hand!

ESTRAGON. Take it!

VLADIMIR. Come to my arms!

ESTRAGON. Your arms?

VLADIMIR. My breast!

ESTRAGON. Off we go!

They embrace. They separate. Silence.

VLADIMIR. How time flies when one has fun!

Silence.

ESTRAGON. What do we do now?

VLADIMIR. While waiting.

ESTRAGON. While waiting.

Silence.

VLADIMIR. We could do our exercises.

ESTRAGON. Our movements.

VLADIMIR. Our elevations.

ESTRAGON. Our relaxations.

VLADIMIR. Our elongations.

ESTRAGON. Our relaxations.

VLADIMIR. To warm us up.

ESTRAGON. To calm us down.

VLADIMIR. Off we go.

> *Vladimir hops from one foot to the other.*
> *Estragon imitates him.*

ESTRAGON *(stopping).* That's enough. I'm tired.

VLADIMIR *(stopping).* We're not in form. What about a little deep
> breathing?

ESTRAGON. I'm tired breathing.

VLADIMIR. You're right. *(Pause.)* Let's just do the tree, [1] for the
> balance.

ESTRAGON. The tree?

> *Vladimir does the tree, staggering about on one leg.*

VLADIMIR *(stopping).* Your turn.

> *Estragon does the tree, staggers.*

ESTRAGON. Do you think God sees me?

VLADIMIR. You must close your eyes.

> *Estragon closes his eyes, staggers worse.*

ESTRAGON *(stopping, brandishing his fists, [2] at the top of his voice).*
> God have pity on me!

VLADIMIR *(vexed).* And me?

ESTRAGON. On me! On me! Pity! On me!

---

1. *do the tree* : do a gymnastic exercise involving standing on one
   leg and stretching out the arms like the branches of a tree. Alan
   Schneider wrote that Beckett did not intend the exercise to be a
   representation of the tree on the stage but one of the basic
   positions in yoga 'in which the sole of one foot is placed directly
   alongside the calf of the other, with the two hands clasped
   together as if in prayer'.
2. *brandishing his fists* : shaking his fists as if they are weapons.

Enter Pozzo and Lucky. [1] *Pozzo is blind. Lucky burdened as before. Rope as before, but much shorter, so that Pozzo may follow more easily. Lucky wearing a different hat. At the sight of Vladimir and Estragon he stops short. Pozzo, continuing on his way, bumps into him.*

VLADIMIR. Gogo!

POZZO (*clutching on to Lucky who staggers*). What is it? Who is it?

Lucky falls, drops everything and brings down Pozzo with him. They lie helpless among the scattered baggage.

ESTRAGON. Is it Godot?

VLADIMIR. At last! (*He goes towards the heap.*) Reinforcements at last!

POZZO. Help!

ESTRAGON. Is it Godot?

VLADIMIR. We were beginning to weaken. Now we're sure to see the evening out.

POZZO. Help!

ESTRAGON. Do you hear him?

VLADIMIR. We are no longer alone, waiting for the night, waiting for Godot, waiting for... waiting. All evening we have struggled, unassisted. Now it's over. It's already tomorrow.

POZZO. Help!

VLADIMIR. Time flows again already. The sun will set, the moon will rise, and we away... from here.

1. *Enter Pozzo and Lucky* : Beckett wrote as follows to the writers of *A Student's Guide to the Plays of Samuel Beckett* (Faber, 1978): ' "In all productions of Godot I have had anything to do with P. and L. in Act 2 come in from the opposite side. This for me is correct. They go to and fro." In conversation he said that they were returning from the fair, 'and added half-jokingly that Pozzo hadn't been able to find a buyer for Lucky' (*Student's Guide*, pp. 67-8).

POZZO. Pity!

VLADIMIR. Poor Pozzo!

ESTRAGON. I knew it was him.

VLADIMIR. Who?

ESTRAGON. Godot.

VLADIMIR. But it's not Godot.

ESTRAGON. It's not Godot?

VLADIMIR. It's not Godot.

ESTRAGON. Then who is it?

VLADIMIR. It's Pozzo.

POZZO. Here! Here! Help me up!

VLADIMIR. He can't get up.

ESTRAGON. Let's go.

VLADIMIR. We can't.

ESTRAGON. Why not?

VLADIMIR. We're waiting for Godot.

ESTRAGON. Ah!

VLADIMIR. Perhaps he has another bone for you.

ESTRAGON. Bone?

VLADIMIR. Chicken. Do you not remember?

ESTRAGON. It was him?

VLADIMIR. Yes.

ESTRAGON. Ask him.

VLADIMIR. Perhaps we should help him first.

ESTRAGON. To do what?

VLADIMIR. To get up.

ESTRAGON. He can't get up?

VLADIMIR. He wants to get up.

ESTRAGON. Then let him get up.

VLADIMIR. He can't.

ESTRAGON. Why not?

VLADIMIR. I don't know.

Pozzo writhes, groans, beats the ground with his fists.

ESTRAGON. We should ask him for the bone first. Then if he refuses we'll leave him there.

VLADIMIR. You mean we have him at our mercy?

ESTRAGON. Yes.

VLADIMIR. And that we should subordinate our good offices to certain conditions.

ESTRAGON. What?

VLADIMIR. That seems intelligent all right. But there's one thing I'm afraid of.

POZZO. Help!

ESTRAGON. What?

VLADIMIR. That Lucky might get going all of a sudden. Then we'd be ballocksed. [1]

ESTRAGON. Lucky?

VLADIMIR. He's the one who went for you yesterday.

ESTRAGON. I tell you there was ten of them.

VLADIMIR. No, before that, the one that kicked you.

ESTRAGON. Is he there?

VLADIMIR. As large as life. *(Gesture towards Lucky.)* For the moment he is inert. But he might run amuck [2] any minute.

POZZO. Help!

---

1. *ballocksed* : finished, done for, castrated (based on 'ballocks', the vulgar word for testicles).
2. *run amuck* : rush about in a wild and angry frenzy (more often 'run amok').

ESTRAGON. And suppose we gave him a good beating, the two of
          us?

VLADIMIR. You mean if we fell on [1] him in his sleep?

ESTRAGON. Yes.

VLADIMIR. That seems a good idea all right. But could we do it? Is
          he really asleep? *(Pause.)* No, the best would be to
          take advantage of Pozzo's calling for help—

POZZO. Help!

VLADIMIR. To help him—

ESTRAGON. We help him?

VLADIMIR. In anticipation of some tangible return.

ESTRAGON. And suppose he—

VLADIMIR. Let us not waste our time in idle [2] discourse! *(Pause.
          Vehemently.)* Let us do something, while we have the
          chance! It is not every day that we are needed. Not
          indeed that we personally are needed. Others would
          meet the case equally well, if not better. To all
          mankind they were addressed, those cries for help
          still ringing in our ears! But at this place, at this
          moment of time, all mankind is us, whether we like it
          or not. Let us make the most of it, before it is too late!
          Let us represent worthily for once the foul brood [3] to
          which a cruel fate consigned us! What do you say?
          (Estragon says nothing.) It is true that when with
          folded arms we weigh the pros and cons we are no
          less a credit to our species. The tiger bounds [4] to the
          help of his congeners [5] without the least reflection, or

1. *fell on* : attacked.
2. *idle* ['ʌɪdəl] : pointless, useless.
3. *foul brood* : disgusting family, i.e. the human race.
4. *bounds* : jumps, leaps.
5. *his congeners* ['kɒndʒɪnəʒ] : those of the same kind or species, i.e.
   other tigers.

else he slinks away [1] into the depths of the thickets. [2]
But that is not the question. What are we doing here,
that is the question. And we are blessed in this, that
we happen to know the answer. Yes, in this immense
confusion one thing alone is clear. We are waiting for
Godot to come—

ESTRAGON. Ah!

POZZO. Help!

VLADIMIR. Or for night to fall. *(Pause.)* We have kept our
appointment, and that's an end to that. We are not
saints, but we have kept our appointment. How
many people can boast as much?

ESTRAGON. Billions.

VLADIMIR. You think so?

ESTRAGON. I don't know.

VLADIMIR. You may be right.

POZZO. Help!

VLADIMIR. All I know is that the hours are long, under these
conditions, and constrain us to beguile them with
proceedings which—how shall I say—which may at
first sight seem reasonable, until they become a habit.
You may say it is to prevent our reason from
foundering. [3] No doubt. But has it not long been
straying [4] in the night without end of the abyssal
depths? That's what I sometimes wonder. You follow
my reasoning?

ESTRAGON *(aphoristic for once)*. We all are born mad. Some remain
so.

---

1. *slinks away* : goes away in an ashamed manner.
2. *thickets* ['θɪkɪts] : shrubs, trees, etc. growing close together.
3. *foundering* : collapsing, failing.
4. *straying* : wandering lost.

POZZO. Help! I'll pay you!

ESTRAGON. How much?

POZZO. One hundred francs!

ESTRAGON. It's not enough.

VLADIMIR. I wouldn't go so far as that.

ESTRAGON. You think it's enough?

VLADIMIR. No, I mean so far as to assert that I was weak in the head when I came into the world. But that is not the question.

POZZO. Two hundred!

VLADIMIR. We wait. We are bored. *(He throws up his hand.)* No, don't protest, we are bored to death, there's no denying it. Good. A diversion comes along and what do we do? We let it go to waste. Come, let's get to work! *(He advances towards the heap, stops in his stride.)* In an instant all will vanish and we'll be alone once more, in the midst of nothingness!

He broods.

POZZO. Two hundred!

VLADIMIR. We're coming!

He tries to pull Pozzo to his feet, fails, tries again, stumbles,[1] *falls, tries to get up, fails.*

ESTRAGON. What's the matter with you all?

VLADIMIR. Help!

ESTRAGON. I'm going.

VLADIMIR. Don't leave me! They'll kill me!

POZZO. Where am I?

VLADIMIR. Gogo!

---

1. *stumbles* : almost falls.

POZZO. Help!

VLADIMIR. Help!

ESTRAGON. I'm going.

VLADIMIR. Help me up first. Then we'll go together.

ESTRAGON. You promise?

VLADIMIR. I swear it!

ESTRAGON. And we'll never come back?

VLADIMIR. Never!

ESTRAGON. We'll go to the Pyrenees.

VLADIMIR. Wherever you like.

ESTRAGON. I've always wanted to wander in the Pyrenees.

VLADIMIR. You'll wander in them.

ESTRAGON *(recoiling)*. Who farted?

VLADIMIR. Pozzo.

POZZO. Here! Here! Pity!

ESTRAGON. It's revolting!

VLADIMIR. Quick! Give me your hand.

ESTRAGON. I'm going. *(Pause. Louder.)* I'm going.

VLADIMIR. Well I suppose in the end I'll get up by myself. *(He tries, fails.)* In the fullness of time.

ESTRAGON. What's the matter with you?

VLADIMIR. Go to hell.

ESTRAGON. Are you staying there?

VLADIMIR. For the time being.

ESTRAGON. Come on, get up, you'll catch a chill.

VLADIMIR. Don't worry about me.

ESTRAGON. Come on, Didi, don't be pig-headed.

> *He stretches out his hand which Vladimir makes haste to seize.*

VLADIMIR. Pull!

> *Estragon pulls, stumbles, falls. Long silence.*

POZZO. Help!

VLADIMIR. We've arrived.

POZZO. Who are you?

VLADIMIR. We are men.

> *Silence.*

ESTRAGON. Sweet mother earth!

VLADIMIR. Can you get up?

ESTRAGON. I don't know.

VLADIMIR. Try.

ESTRAGON. Not now, not now.

> *Silence.*

POZZO. What happened?

VLADIMIR *(violently)*. Will you stop it, you! Pest! He thinks of
> nothing but himself!

ESTRAGON. What about a little snooze?[1]

VLADIMIR. Did you hear him? He wants to know what happened!

ESTRAGON. Don't mind him. Sleep.

> *Silence.*

POZZO. Pity! Pity!

ESTRAGON *(with a start)*. What is it?

VLADIMIR. Were you asleep?

ESTRAGON. I must have been.

VLADIMIR. It's this bastard Pozzo at it again.

---

1. *a little snooze* : a short sleep.

ESTRAGON. Make him stop it. Kick him in the crotch. [1]

VLADIMIR *(striking Pozzo).* Will you stop it! Crablouse! [2] *(Pozzo extricates himself with cries of pain and crawls away. He stops, saws the air blindly, [3] calling for help. Vladimir, propped [4] on his elbow, observes his retreat.)* He's off! *(Pozzo collapses.)* He's down!

ESTRAGON. What do we do now?

VLADIMIR. Perhaps I could crawl to him.

ESTRAGON. Don't leave me!

VLADIMIR. Or I could call to him.

ESTRAGON. Yes, call to him.

VLADIMIR. Pozzo! *(Silence.)* Pozzo! *(Silence.)* No reply.

ESTRAGON. Together.

ESTRAGON.
VLADIMIR. } Pozzo! Pozzo!

VLADIMIR. He moved.

ESTRAGON. Are you sure his name is Pozzo?

VLADIMIR *(alarmed).* Mr. Pozzo! Come back! We won't hurt you!

    Silence.

ESTRAGON. We might try him with other names.

VLADIMIR. I'm afraid he's dying.

ESTRAGON. It'd be amusing.

VLADIMIR. What'd be amusing?

1. *crotch* : place where human legs fork.
2. *Crablouse* : parasitical insect infesting the human body.
3. *saws the air blindly* : in his blindness waves his hands around in an uncontrolled manner.
4. *propped* : holding himself up.

ESTRAGON. To try with other names, one after the other. It'd pass
the time. And we'd be bound [1] to hit on the right one
sooner or later.

VLADIMIR. I tell you his name is Pozzo.

ESTRAGON. We'll soon see. *(He reflects.)* Abel! Abel!

POZZO. Help!

ESTRAGON. Got it in one!

VLADIMIR. I begin to weary of this motif.

ESTRAGON. Perhaps the other is called Cain. Cain! Cain!

POZZO. Help!

ESTRAGON. He's all humanity. *(Silence.)* Look at the little cloud.

VLADIMIR *(raising his eyes).* Where?

ESTRAGON. There. In the zenith.

VLADIMIR. Well? *(Pause.)* What is there so wonderful about it?

   Silence.

ESTRAGON. Let's pass on now to something else, do you mind?

VLADIMIR. I was just going to suggest it.

ESTRAGON. But to what?

VLADIMIR. Ah!

   Silence.

ESTRAGON. Suppose we got up to begin with.

VLADIMIR. No harm in trying.

   They get up.

ESTRAGON. Child's play.

VLADIMIR. Simple question of will-power.

ESTRAGON. And now?

---

1. *we'd be bound* : we'd be sure.

POZZO. Help!

ESTRAGON. Let's go.

VLADIMIR. We can't.

ESTRAGON. Why not?

VLADIMIR. We're waiting for Godot.

ESTRAGON. Ah! *(Despairing.)* What'll we do, what'll we do!

POZZO. Help!

VLADIMIR. What about helping him?

ESTRAGON. What does he want?

VLADIMIR. He wants to get up.

ESTRAGON. Then why doesn't he?

VLADIMIR. He wants us to help him to get up.

ESTRAGON. Then why don't we? What are we waiting for?

> *They help Pozzo to his feet, let him go. He falls.*

VLADIMIR. We must hold him. *(They get him up again. Pozzo sags between them, his arms round their necks.)* Feeling better?

POZZO. Who are you?

VLADIMIR. Do you not recognize us?

POZZO. I am blind.

> *Silence.*

ESTRAGON. Perhaps he can see into the future. [1]

VLADIMIR. Since when?

POZZO. I used to have wonderful sight—but are you friends?

ESTRAGON *(laughing noisily)*. He wants to know if we are friends!

---

1. *Perhaps he can see into the future* : Possibly an allusion to the idea that the blind were supposed to have prophetic powers, like those of Tiresias in Sophocles' *Oedipus the King*.

VLADIMIR. No, he means friends of his.

ESTRAGON. Well?

VLADIMIR. We've proved we are, by helping him.

ESTRAGON. Exactly. Would we have helped him if we weren't his
friends?

VLADIMIR. Possibly.

ESTRAGON. True.

VLADIMIR. Don't let's quibble [1] about that now.

POZZO. You are not highwaymen? [2]

ESTRAGON. Highwaymen! Do we look like highwaymen?

VLADIMIR. Damn it, can't you see the man is blind!

ESTRAGON. Damn it, so he is. *(Pause.)* So he says.

POZZO. Don't leave me!

VLADIMIR. No question of it.

ESTRAGON. For the moment.

POZZO. What time is it?

VLADIMIR *(inspecting the sky).* Seven o'clock... eight o'clock...

ESTRAGON. That depends what time of year it is.

POZZO. Is it evening?

> *Silence. Vladimir and Estragon scrutinize the sunset.*

ESTRAGON. It's rising.

VLADIMIR. Impossible.

ESTRAGON. Perhaps it's the dawn.

VLADIMIR. Don't be a fool. It's the west over there.

ESTRAGON. How do you know?

POZZO *(anguished).* Is it evening?

---

1. *quibble* : argue.
2. *highwaymen* : thieves who rob travellers.

VLADIMIR. Anyway it hasn't moved.

ESTRAGON. I tell you it's rising.

POZZO. Why don't you answer me?

ESTRAGON. Give us a chance.

VLADIMIR *(reassuring)*. It's evening, sir, it's evening, night is
drawing nigh. [1] My friend here would have me doubt
it [2] and I must confess he shook me [3] for a moment.
But it is not for nothing I have lived through this long
day and I can assure you it is very near the end of its
repertory. *(Pause.)* How do you feel now?

ESTRAGON. How much longer must we cart him round? *(They half
release him, catch him again as he falls.)* We are not
caryatids!

VLADIMIR. You were saying your sight used to be good, if I heard
you right.

POZZO. Wonderful! Wonderful, wonderful sight!

   Silence.

ESTRAGON *(irritably)*. Expand! Expand!

VLADIMIR. Let him alone. Can't you see he's thinking of the days
when he was happy? *(Pause.)* Memoria praeteritorum
bonorum— [4] that must be unpleasant.

ESTRAGON. We wouldn't know.

VLADIMIR. And it came on you all of a sudden?

POZZO. Quite wonderful!

VLADIMIR. I'm asking you if it came on you all of a sudden.

---

1. *night is drawing nigh (near)* : the second line of the hymn 'Now
    the day is over', by S. Baring-Gould, also quoted in *Krapp's Last
    Tape.*
2. *would have me doubt it* : wants me to doubt it.
3. *shook me* : made me have doubts, confused me.
4. *Memoria praeteritorum bonorum* : memory of past happiness.

POZZO. I woke up one fine day as blind as Fortune. *(Pause.)*
　　Sometimes I wonder if I'm not still asleep.

VLADIMIR. And when was that?

POZZO. I don't know.

VLADIMIR. But no later than yesterday—

POZZO *(violently)*. Don't question me! The blind have no notion of
　　time. The things of time are hidden from them too.

VLADIMIR. Well just fancy that! I could have sworn it was just the
　　opposite.

ESTRAGON. I'm going.

POZZO. Where are we?

VLADIMIR. I couldn't tell you.

POZZO. It isn't by any chance the place known as the Board? [1]

VLADIMIR. Never heard of it.

POZZO. What is it like?

VLADIMIR *(looking round)*. It's indescribable. It's like nothing.
　　There's nothing. There's a tree.

POZZO. Then it's not the Board.

ESTRAGON *(sagging)*. Some diversion!

POZZO. Where is my menial? [2]

VLADIMIR. He's about somewhere.

POZZO. Why doesn't he answer when I call?

VLADIMIR. I don't know. He seems to be sleeping. Perhaps he's
　　dead.

POZZO. What happened exactly?

ESTRAGON. Exactly!

VLADIMIR. The two of you slipped. *(Pause.)* And fell.

---

1. *the Board* : may be a reference to the stage (actors are said to
　　tread the boards).
2. *menial* : servant.

POZZO. Go and see is he hurt.

VLADIMIR. We can't leave you.

POZZO. You needn't both go.

VLADIMIR *(to Estragon)*. You go.

ESTRAGON. After what he did to me? Never!

POZZO. Yes yes, let your friend go, he stinks so. *(Silence.)* What is he waiting for?

VLADIMIR. What are you waiting for?

ESTRAGON. I'm waiting for Godot.

   Silence.

VLADIMIR. What exactly should he do?

POZZO. Well to begin with he should pull on the rope, as hard as he likes so long as he doesn't strangle him. He usually responds to that. If not he should give him a taste of his boot, in the face and the privates [1] as far as possible.

VLADIMIR *(to Estragon)*. You see, you've nothing to be afraid of. It's even an opportunity to revenge yourself.

ESTRAGON. And if he defends himself?

POZZO. No no, he never defends himself.

VLADIMIR. I'll come flying to the rescue.

ESTRAGON. Don't take your eyes off me.

   He goes towards Lucky.

VLADIMIR. Make sure he's alive before you start. No point in exerting yourself if he's dead.

ESTRAGON *(bending over Lucky)*. He's breathing.

VLADIMIR. Then let him have it.

---

   1. *the privates* : the genitals.

With sudden fury Estragon starts kicking Lucky, hurling abuse[1] at him as he does so. But he hurts his foot and moves away limping and groaning. Lucky stirs.

ESTRAGON. Oh the brute!

He sits down on the mound and tries to take off his boot. But he soon desists and disposes himself for sleep, his arms on his knees and his head on his arms.

POZZO. What's gone wrong now?

VLADIMIR. My friend has hurt himself.

POZZO. And Lucky?

VLADIMIR. So it is he?

POZZO. What?

VLADIMIR. It is Lucky?

POZZO. I don't understand.

VLADIMIR. And you are Pozzo?

POZZO. Certainly I am Pozzo.

VLADIMIR. The same as yesterday?

POZZO. Yesterday?

VLADIMIR. We met yesterday. *(Silence.)* Do you not remember?

POZZO. I don't remember having met anyone yesterday. But tomorrow I won't remember having met anyone today. So don't count on me to enlighten you.

VLADIMIR. But—

POZZO. Enough. Up pig!

VLADIMIR. You were bringing him to the fair to sell him. You spoke to us. He danced. He thought. You had your sight.

---

1. *hurling* [həːlɪŋ] *abuse* : shouting abuse (hurling = throwing violently).

POZZO. As you please. Let me go! *(Vladimir moves away.)* Up!

> *Lucky gets up, gathers up* [1] *his burdens.*

VLADIMIR. Where do you go from here?

POZZO. On. *(Lucky, laden down,* [2] *takes his place before Pozzo.)* Whip!
(Lucky puts everything down, looks for whip, finds it, puts it into Pozzo's hand, takes up everything again.) Rope!

> *Lucky puts everything down, puts end of the rope into Pozzo's hand, takes up everything again.*

VLADIMIR. What is there in the bag?

POZZO. Sand. *(He jerks the rope.)* On!

VLADIMIR. Don't go yet!

POZZO. I'm going.

VLADIMIR. What do you do when you fall far from help?

POZZO. We wait till we can get up. Then we go on. On!

VLADIMIR. Before you go tell him to sing!

POZZO. Who?

VLADIMIR. Lucky.

POZZO. To sing?

VLADIMIR. Yes. Or to think. Or to recite.

POZZO. But he's dumb.

VLADIMIR. Dumb!

POZZO. Dumb. He can't even groan.

VLADIMIR. Dumb! Since when?

POZZO *(suddenly furious).* Have you not done tormenting me with your accursed time! It's abominable! When! When! One day, is that not enough for you, one day like any

---

1. *gathers up* : picks up.
2. *laden down* : bending under the heavy weight with which he is loaded.

other day, one day he went dumb, one day I went blind, one day we'll go deaf, one day we were born, one day we shall die, the same day, the same second, is that not enough for you? *(Calmer.)* They give birth astride of [1] a grave, the light gleams [2] an instant, then it's night once more. *(He jerks the rope.)* On!

Exeunt Pozzo and Lucky. Vladimir follows them to the edge of the stage, looks after them. The noise of falling, reinforced by mimic of Vladimir, announces that they are down again. Silence. Vladimir goes towards Estragon, contemplates him a moment, then shakes him awake.

ESTRAGON *(wild gestures, incoherent words. Finally).* Why will you never let me sleep?

VLADIMIR. I felt lonely.

ESTRAGON. I was dreaming I was happy.

VLADIMIR. That passed the time.

ESTRAGON. I was dreaming that—

VLADIMIR *(violently).* Don't tell me! *(Silence.)* I wonder is he really blind.

ESTRAGON. Blind? Who?

VLADIMIR. Pozzo.

ESTRAGON. Blind?

VLADIMIR. He told us he was blind.

ESTRAGON. Well what about it?

VLADIMIR. It seemed to me he saw us.

ESTRAGON. You dreamt it. *(Pause.)* Let's go. We can't. Ah! *(Pause.)* Are you sure it wasn't him?

VLADIMIR. Who?

ESTRAGON. Godot.

1. *astride of* : with their legs open across.
2. *gleams* : shines intensely.

VLADIMIR. But who?

ESTRAGON. Pozzo.

VLADIMIR. Not at all! *(Less sure.)* Not at all! *(Still less sure.)* Not at all!

ESTRAGON. I suppose I might as well get up. *(He gets up painfully.)* Ow! Didi!

VLADIMIR. I don't know what to think any more.

ESTRAGON. My feet! *(He sits down, tries to take off his boots.)* Help me!

VLADIMIR. Was I sleeping, while the others suffered? Am I sleeping now? Tomorrow, when I wake, or think I do, what shall I say of today? That with Estragon my friend, at this place, until the fall of night, I waited for Godot? That Pozzo passed, with his carrier, and that he spoke to us? Probably. But in all that what truth will there be? *(Estragon, having struggled with his boots in vain, is dozing off again. Vladimir stares at him.)* He'll know nothing. He'll tell me about the blows he received and I'll give him a carrot. *(Pause.)* Astride of a grave and a difficult birth. Down in the hole, lingeringly, [1] the grave-digger puts on the forceps. We have time to grow old. The air is full of our cries. *(He listens.)* But habit is a great deadener. *(He looks again at Estragon.)* At me too someone is looking, of me too someone is saying, he is sleeping, he knows nothing, let him sleep on. *(Pause.)* I can't go on! *(Pause.)* What have I said?

He goes feverishly to and fro, halts finally at extreme left, broods. Enter Boy right. He halts. Silence.

BOY. Mister… *(Vladimir turns.)* Mr. Albert…

VLADIMIR. Off we go again. *(Pause.)* Do you not recognize me?

---

1. *lingeringly* : without hurrying.

BOY. No, sir.

VLADIMIR. It wasn't you came yesterday.

BOY. No, sir.

VLADIMIR. This is your first time.

BOY. Yes, sir.

> *Silence.*

VLADIMIR. You have a message from Mr. Godot.

BOY. Yes, sir.

VLADIMIR. He won't come this evening.

BOY. No, sir.

VLADIMIR. But he'll come tomorrow.

BOY. Yes, sir.

VLADIMIR. Without fail.

BOY. Yes, sir.

> *Silence.*

VLADIMIR. Did you meet anyone?

BOY. No, sir.

VLADIMIR. Two other... *(he hesitates)*... men?

BOY. I didn't see anyone, sir.

> *Silence.*

VLADIMIR. What does he do, Mr. Godot? *(Silence.)* Do you hear me?

BOY. Yes, sir.

VLADIMIR. Well?

BOY. He does nothing, sir.

> *Silence.*

VLADIMIR. How is your brother?

BOY. He's sick, sir.

VLADIMIR. Perhaps it was he came yesterday.

BOY. I don't know, sir.

Silence.

VLADIMIR *(softly)*. Has he a beard, Mr. Godot?

BOY. Yes, sir.

VLADIMIR. Fair or… *(he hesitates)*… or black?

BOY. I think it's white, sir. [1]

Silence.

VLADIMIR. Christ have mercy on us!

Silence.

BOY. What am I to tell Mr. Godot, sir?

VLADIMIR. Tell him… *(he hesitates)*… tell him you saw me and that… *(he hesitates)*… that you saw me. *(Pause. Vladimir advances, the Boy recoils. Vladimir halts, the Boy halts. With sudden violence.)* You're sure you saw me, you won't come and tell me tomorrow that you never saw me!

Silence. Vladimir makes a sudden spring [2] forward, the Boy avoids him and exit running. Silence. The sun sets, the moon rises. As in Act I. Vladimir stands motionless and bowed. [3] Estragon wakes, takes off his boots, gets up with one in each hand and goes and puts them down centre front, then goes towards Vladimir.

ESTRAGON. What's wrong with you?

VLADIMIR. Nothing.

---

1. *I think it's white, sir* : The writers of *A Student's Guide* tell us: 'According to Mr Beckett, the whiteness shows Vladimir that Godot is very old: "if he were less experienced there might be some hope.", See also p. 116

2. *spring* : jump.

3. *bowed* [baʊd] : with his head lowered and his body bent.

ESTRAGON. I'm going.

VLADIMIR. So am I.

ESTRAGON. Was I long asleep?

VLADIMIR. I don't know.

Silence.

ESTRAGON. Where shall we go?

VLADIMIR. Not far.

ESTRAGON. Oh yes, let's go far away from here.

VLADIMIR. We can't.

ESTRAGON. Why not?

VLADIMIR. We have to come back tomorrow.

ESTRAGON. What for?

VLADIMIR. To wait for Godot.

ESTRAGON. Ah! *(Silence.)* He didn't come?

VLADIMIR. No.

ESTRAGON. And now it's too late.

VLADIMIR. Yes, now it's night.

ESTRAGON. And if we dropped him?[1] *(Pause.)* If we dropped him?

VLADIMIR. He'd punish us. *(Silence. He looks at the tree.)* Everything's
            dead but the tree.

ESTRAGON *(looking at the tree).* What is it?

VLADIMIR. It's the tree.

ESTRAGON. Yes, but what kind?

VLADIMIR. I don't know. A willow.[2]

---

1. *dropped him* : broke off acquaintance with him. People are said to
   'drop' their social inferiors; given their low social status, the idea
   of Vladimir and Estragon dropping people is comical.
2. *willow* : traditionally called the weeping willow and so associated
   with tears.

Estragon draws Vladimir towards the tree. They stand motionless before it. Silence.

ESTRAGON. Why don't we hang ourselves?

VLADIMIR. With what?

ESTRAGON. You haven't got a bit of rope?

VLADIMIR. No.

ESTRAGON. Then we can't.

Silence

VLADIMIR. Let's go.

ESTRAGON. Wait, there's my belt.

VLADIMIR. It's too short.

ESTRAGON. You could hang on to my legs.

VLADIMIR. And who'd hang on to mine?

ESTRAGON. True.

VLADIMIR. Show all the same. *(Estragon loosens the cord that holds up his trousers which, much too big for him, fall about his ankles.* [1] *They look at the cord.)* It might do at a pinch. [2] But is it strong enough?

ESTRAGON. We'll soon see. Here.

They each take an end of the cord and pull. It breaks. They almost fall.

VLADIMIR. Not worth a curse.

Silence.

---

1. *fall about his ankles* : To Pierre Latour, the first Estragon, this piece of business lacked dignity. But in a letter to Blin of 9 January, 1953, Beckett insists on the necessity of the routine, explaining that nothing is more comical than the tragic (these words are similar to those of Nell in *Endgame*, when she says that 'nothing is funnier than unhappiness').

2. *at a pinch* : as there is nothing better.

ESTRAGON. You say we have to come back tomorrow?

VLADIMIR. Yes.

ESTRAGON. Then we can bring a good bit of rope.

VLADIMIR. Yes.

    Silence.

ESTRAGON. Didi.

VLADIMIR. Yes.

ESTRAGON. I can't go on like this.

VLADIMIR. That's what you think.

ESTRAGON. If we parted? That might be better for us.

VLADIMIR. We'll hang ourselves tomorrow. *(Pause.)* Unless Godot
        comes.

ESTRAGON. And if he comes?

VLADIMIR. We'll be saved.

    *Vladimir takes off his hat (Lucky's), peers inside it, feels about
    inside it, shakes it, knocks on the crown, puts it on again.*

ESTRAGON. Well? Shall we go?

VLADIMIR. Pull on your trousers.

ESTRAGON. What?

VLADIMIR. Pull on your trousers.

ESTRAGON. You want me to pull off my trousers?

VLADIMIR. Pull ON your trousers.

ESTRAGON *(realizing his trousers are down)*. True.

    He pulls up his trousers.

VLADIMIR. Well? Shall we go?

ESTRAGON. Yes, let's go.

    They do not move.

CURTAIN

ACTIVITIES

Comprehension Questions

Beginning of act to p. 95, Vladimir sighs deeply.

1. What might be agitating Vladimir at the beginning of the act?

2. In what way is Vladimir's song appropriate to the play and its action?

3. What aspects of the situation and the characters are the same as in Act 1? (pp. 90-3) What has changed? What significance could be attached to the change(s)?

4. 'Don't touch me! Don't question me! Don't speak to me! Stay with me!'
   How do you interpret this speech of Estragon? (p. 91)

5. 'One isn't master of one's moods.' Find stage directions indicating Vladimir's frequent shifts of mood. (pp. 89-93)

6. What do Estragon's words and the stage directions indicate of his mood? (pp. 90-2)

7. How is uncertainty again suggested in these opening pages of Act 2?

8. How does Estragon's language reflect his mood on pp. 94-5?

9. Summarise this section.

Pages 95-100:
Vladimir: 'You're a hard man to get on with, Gogo'... Silence.

1. Estragon says, 'The best thing would be to kill me, like the other.' What other could he be referring to? (p. 96)

2. Why do Vladimir and Estragon wish so desperately to keep on talking?

3. What are 'all the dead voices'? (pp. 96-7)

4. What do they suggest doing to try to avoid silence? Which suggestion is rejected? (pp. 96-100)

5. On p. 98 Vladimir repeats again that they have to wait for Godot. What is the cumulative effect of these repetitions (which will continue throughout the play)?

6. Look at these two remarks by Vladimir on p. 99:
   'Thinking is not the worst.'
   'What is terrible is to have thought.'
   How far do the two statements contradict each other?

7. When the tramps speak of 'corpses' and 'skeletons', what are they referring to? (p. 99)

8. What image is used for the human mind on p. 99?

9. If to have thought is not the worst (p. 99), what might the worst have been?

10. What does 'Que voulez-vous?' mean (p. 100)?

11. Summarise this section.

A C T I V I T I E S

Pages 100-4:
Estragon: 'That wasn't a bad little canter' . . . Estragon: 'Not enough.'
Silence.

1. 'That wasn't a bad little canter.' What is Estragon referring to?

2. How is uncertainty again suggested in this section of the text?

3. On p. 100 Vladimir says he is not a historian. What does this suggest?

4. 'There's no lack of void.' (p. 101) What does Estragon mean?

5. What does the word 'blathered' tell us about Estragon's opinion of the tramps' activities the previous evening and for the previous half a century? (p. 101)

6. How does Vladimir try to convince Estragon that they were in the same place the previous evening? (pp. 100-3)

7. Which of the two said 'What'll we do?' in Act 1? How is the despair intensified here? (p. 104)

8. On p. 104, how is the tramps' reduction in circumstances suggested?

9. When Vladimir says 'This is really becoming insignificant', Estragon replies, 'Not enough.' What does he mean by this? (p. 104)

10. Summarise this section.

Pages 104-7:
Vladimir: 'What about trying them?' . . . to keep himself warm.

1. On p. 105 Estragon says, 'I've tried everything.' What attempts might he be referring to?

2. Why do you think Estragon insists on the word 'relaxation', rejecting Vladimir's words 'occupation' and 'recreation'? (p. 105)

3. Why does Vladimir say 'Yes yes, we're magicians'? (p. 105)

4. Whose way of speaking does Vladimir echo in the speech beginning, 'Yes, yes, we're magicians'?

5. Why should Estragon so vehemently reject the idea of laces? (p. 105)

6. Summarise this section.

Pages 107-9:
Estragon wakes with a start . . . Estragon: 'I'm going.' Silence.

1. How is Estragon's increasingly despairing mood conveyed? (pp. 107-8)

2. What convinces Vladimir that they have come to the right place? (p. 108)

3. What is the dramatic function of the 'three hats for two heads' comic routine? (pp. 108-9)

4. Summarise this section.

ACTIVITIES

Pages 110-12:
Vladimir: Will you not play? . . . They resume their watch. Silence.

1. What is amusing about Estragon's cursing of Vladimir?

2. Contrast Vladimir's behaviour with Estragon's in this section of the text.

3. Why does Estragon recoil in horror? (p. 111)

4. Summarise this section.

Pages 112-15:
Vladimir: 'You must have had a vision' . . . Estragon: 'On me! On me! Pity! On me!'

1. How do the two tramps pass the time in this sequence? Summarise the sequence, indicating its comic moments.

2. At what moment does the tone become suddenly serious?

Pages 116-21:
Enter Pozzo and Lucky . . . stumbles, falls, tries to get up, fails.

1. In what way has Pozzo changed?

2. In what different ways do the two tramps react to the appearance of Pozzo and Lucky?

3. How is the difference between the desire and the inability to act shown in this scene? (pp. 116-18)

A C T I V I T I E S

4. What is the attitude of the two tramps to the incapacitated Pozzo at this point in the play? (p. 118)

5. What are Vladimir's feelings about Lucky at this point? (pp. 118-19)

6. What is the contrast between Vladimir's rhetoric about helping others and his (and Estragon's) attitude to Pozzo at this moment? (pp. 119-20)

7. Explain Vladimir's remarks on habit. (p. 120)

8. Summarise this section.

Pages 121-5:
Estragon: 'What's the matter with you all?' ... Vladimir: 'Ah!' Silence.

1. Which tramp is now dependent on the other? (pp. 121-2)

2. How is the gap between expression of the intention to act and action itself again indicated on pp. 121-2?

3. What is ironic about Vladimir's statement: 'We've arrived'? (p. 123)

4. What new way of passing the time is suggested by Estragon? (pp. 124-5)

5. Pozzo responds to both names – Abel and Cain. What interpretation can you offer for this?

6. Summarise this section.

ACTIVITIES

Pages 125-31:
Estragon: 'Suppose we got up to begin with' . . . his head on his arms.

1. Who casts doubt on whether Pozzo is really blind?

2. Pozzo says, 'Don't leave me.' In what way does this connect him with the two tramps?

3. How is uncertainty yet again suggested in these pages? (pp. 126-8)

4. What is the effect of Estragon's comment, 'Some diversion!', on p. 129?

5. Estragon says, 'I'm waiting for Godot.' It is Vladimir who has always referred to the waiting for Godot. What significance might there be in this reversal of roles?

6. Summarise this section.

Pages 131-3:
Pozzo: What's gone wrong now? . . . they are down again. Silence.

1. In the dialogue between Pozzo and Vladimir on p. 131, why is the sense of uncertainty even further increased?

2. What new revelation about Lucky occurs on p. 132?

Pages 133-4:
Vladimir goes towards Estragon . . . halts finally at extreme left, broods.

1. What are the two uncertainties in the dialogue between Vladimir and Estragon on pp. 133-4?

2. Vladimir says 'What have I said?' at the end of his monologue. Why does he say this, why is he so agitated, and what might he be brooding about?

Pages 134-6:
Enter Boy right . . . exit running. Silence.

1. 'Off we go again.' What is the implication of Vladimir's remark?

2. How is uncertainty again created in the scene with the boy?

3. Why is Vladimir so insistent that the boy should tell Mr Godot that he saw him?

Pages 136-9:
The sun sets . . . Curtain.

1. What further suggestions of uncertainty are there here?

2. Comment on the comic business with the rope and Estragon's trousers.

3. What difference is there between the end of Act 1 and that of Act 2?

ACTIVITIES

Post-reading Questions

What is *Waiting for Godot* about? Its themes and vision of life

1. What view of life does Vladimir express in his first speech? Has he completely given up hope?

2. How is the theme of uncertainty established right at the beginning of the play?

3. From his description of the way he spent the night, what do we learn about the kind of life Estragon is leading?

4. How many of the following questions can you answer after the first half dozen pages?

    • Who are these people?

    • Where are they precisely?

    • What are they doing and why?

    • When is this meeting taking place?

    • Are they tramps? If so, where did they get their bowler hats?

    • They have just come together, but how long have they been apart?

    • How often and how long have they been together?

    • Who has been beating Estragon, and why?

    • Why do the two men change their moods so often and so quickly?

    What conclusion do you come to after attempting to answer these questions?

A C T I V I T I E S

5. What makes Vladimir feel both relieved and appalled (p. 8)?

6. Why is Vladimir obsessed with the Biblical story of the two thieves? What themes are introduced in the conversation about the two thieves?

7. It is after this conversation about the two thieves that the theme of waiting for Godot is introduced. Why should Beckett choose to introduce this theme at this particular point?

8. What do we learn about the relationship between Godot and the two tramps?

9. Think again about your answers to questions 1 and 2 on pp. 14-16 of the text. Try now to describe more precisely what constitutes the horror of the situation Vladimir and Estragon find themselves in.

10. How are Vladimir and Estragon represented as abject creatures on pp. 19-20?

11. Vladimir's rummaging in his pockets is a comic routine. What serious situation does the comic business symbolise?

12. Read from Estragon: *'Funny, the more you eat the worse it gets'* to *'Nothing to be done'* (pp. 22-3). What does this piece of dialogue tell us of the way Vladimir and Estragon view their situation?

ACTIVITIES

13. Consider the whole sequence of the play from the beginning to the entrance of Pozzo and Lucky. Make notes on the main themes by completing the grid.

THEME	NOTES
Pessimism/optimism	
The hostility of the world	
Uncertainty/unknowingness	
Illusion/reality	
The quality of the tramps' lives	
The horror of their situation	

THEME	NOTES
Suffering	
The theme of waiting	
Time/eternity	
Memory	
Repentance/ salvation/damnation	
Mixture of farce and seriousness as a vision of life	
The nature of Godot and Vladimir and Estragon's relationship with him	

14. What three things about Pozzo make it understandable that Estragon should mistake him for Godot?

15. Give examples of Pozzo's authoritarian behaviour.

ACTIVITIES

16. What political interpretation(s) can be offered to explain the relationship between Pozzo and Lucky? How far do you think political interpretations are relevant here?

17. In the Comprehension section (question 4 on pp. 49-55), you were asked to outline the main argument (if you could find one) of Lucky's monologue. Reconsider that speech now, first reading note 1 on p. 51, and then complete the grid, commenting on what Lucky says on the three themes.

THEME	COMMENT
Indifference of heaven, and divine apathy	
Dwindling and shrinking man	
'the earth abode of stones'	

18. Various Beckett characters, at the moment of facing defeat, renew their resistance to the harshness of life. A famous example occurs at the end of *The Unnamable* when the speaker concludes: '. . . you must go on, I can't go on, I'll go on.'

    a) How does Lucky, at the apparently most despairing moment of his monologue, show this resistance?

    b) What, in this note of resistance, does Lucky have in common with Vladimir and Estragon?

19. How can we relate Lucky's speech to the play as a whole:

    a) in relation to the situation of Vladimir and Estragon;

    b) as regards their relationship with Godot (given the imprecise knowledge we have of that);

    c) in relation to life on earth?

20. After the exit of Pozzo and Lucky, what changes can we recognise in Vladimir and Estragon in comparison with how they were before the entry of the other couple?

21. On p. 59, Vladimir comments on how Pozzo and Lucky have changed. What does this revelation that everything may have occurred before and the debate which follows contribute to the meaning of the play?

22. Why is Vladimir so insistent that the boy should tell Mr Godot that he saw them? What seems the most terrifying possibility of all at this point in the play?

23. What two references after the exit of the boy show that Estragon is thinking about suicide?

24. In what way is the last tableau of Act 1 an image of the main theme of the play?

25. Act 2 is often said to show, in relation to Act 1, a further degeneration. For example, in the opening tableau the boots and the hat, inanimate objects, seem to have taken over the centre of the stage from the human beings. What other signs of decline do you observe in the opening pages of Act 2?

26. Why should the two characters be in a blacker mood than at the beginning of Act 1?

27. What does the passage about the dead voices suggest about human life? In what way does it deepen the tone of the play?

A C T I V I T I E S

28. What indications are there of growing desperation on the part of the two tramps in the section from p. 95 to p. 100?

29. In your opinion is there any significance in the fact that the tree now has four or five leaves (Vladimir says 'it's covered with leaves')?

30. Think again about Estragon's comment, 'There's no lack of void'. What is the thematic importance of this statement in relation to the play as a whole?

31. In the section from p. 100 to p. 104 we find an intensification of despair. In what way is this related to the meaning of the play as a whole?

32. On p. 105 Estragon says: 'We always find something, eh Didi, to give us the impression we exist?' What major theme of the play is suggested here?

33. As their situation becomes more and more desperate, offering no hope of escape for Vladimir and Estragon from their interminable waiting, Beckett introduces the 'three hats for two heads' comic routine. In what way does this routine represent important themes of the play?

34. Comment on the thematic significance of 'doing the tree' (p. 115).

35. After the grotesque attempt to 'do the tree', Estragon shouts 'God have pity on me!' and when Vladimir asks 'And me?' Estragon insists, 'On me! On me! Pity! On me!' In what sense is this a new thematic development?

36. How are the changes in Pozzo and Lucky related to the meaning of the whole play'?

37. On p. 121, Vladimir says, 'In an instant all will vanish and we'll be alone once more, in the midst of nothingness.' Comment on the thematic importance of this statement.

38. It has been said that there is more exaggeration and broad farce in the second scene with Pozzo and Lucky than anywhere else in the play. Study this sequence and describe its exaggeration and broad farce, then say what these contribute to the meaning of the play.

39. When Vladimir and Estragon hold Pozzo up, he 'sags between them, his arms around their necks'. Try to visualise this image and say what it might suggest. How, then, might this image of the sagging Pozzo be connected with a central theme of the play?

40. On p. 129 Pozzo says, 'Sometimes I wonder if I'm not still asleep.' How is this related to some of the central themes of the play?

41. On p. 130 Estragon says, 'I'm waiting for Godot.' Look back to question 35. What is the connection between Estragon's cry there and his answer to Pozzo here?

42. In his final speech, what does Pozzo say about human life in relation to time? How does this speech contribute to the vision of the play?

43. Why does it seem so important to Vladimir to know whether Pozzo is blind?

44. In his meditation on p. 134:

a) What does Vladimir say about human life and the nature of reality?

b) In what way is his monologue a variation on an essential idea of Pozzo's speech on pp. 132-3?

45. What does Vladimir mean when he says, 'But habit is a great deadener'? In what way is this comment related to Beckett's vision of human life as expressed in *Godot*?

46. In the dialogue with the boy, Vladimir asks two questions that were not asked in Act 1. What are they?

47. When the boy tells Vladimir he thinks Godot's beard is white, Vladimir, after a silence, responds: 'Christ have mercy on us!' Look for other references to a Christian view of the world in the final pages of the play. What might be the reason for these Christian references?

48. In Act 1 Vladimir was very concerned that the boy should tell Godot he had seen both Vladimir himself and Estragon. He used the word 'us'. Here he says, 'Tell him . . . (he hesitates) . . . tell him you saw me and that . . . (he hesitates) . . . that you saw me.' Similarly he substitutes 'me' for 'us' in his final words to the boy. Note, too, Vladimir's greater aggressiveness towards the boy. How would you interpret these changes?

49. The closing scene has been said 'to achieve a perfect synthesis of metaphysical desperation and meticulously performed slapstick comedy' (Lawrence Graver). Discuss the scene in the light of this comment. (Slapstick comedy is the kind of farcical comedy associated with circus clowns or with film comedians like Laurel and Hardy.)

50. What image of human life are we left with in the final words and tableau?

51. What are the most important themes in *Waiting for Godot*? Choose from the following list and add any other themes you consider important:

   • fear of the unknown and of silence;
   • identity and the nature of the self;
   • illusion and reality;
   • life and death;
   • man as the victim of unknown forces for reasons unknown;
   • repentance, damnation and salvation;

- suffering;
- the absurdity of existence;
- the unreliability of memory;
- time and eternity;
- uncertainty and unknowingness;
- waiting.

52. Write comments on three of the themes you chose in question 51 and show how each is important to Beckett's central vision in *Waiting for Godot*.

53. From the beginning *Waiting for Godot* has attracted different, indeed contradictory, interpretations. In his edition of the play, published ten years after the first English production, Colin Duckworth was already able to list a dozen different kinds of interpretation. Here are some of them. The play has been seen as:

- dramatic representation of the wretchedness of man without God;

- 'the artistic portrayal of man's absurd existence as it appears to Beckett';

- a revelation of 'man's anguish as he waits for the arrival of something that will give life meaning and bring an end to his suffering';

- 'a profoundly anti-Christian play';

- 'a Christian play';

- 'a modern morality play on permanent Christian themes';

- 'an atheist existentialist play'.

(See Colin Duckworth: *En attendant Godot,* p. xcviii, where the sources of the quotations are acknowledged.)

Offer your interpretation of the play, bearing in mind that definitions of works of art in terms of a single idea tend to be reductive.

ACTIVITIES

Who is Godot, and does it matter?

1. Having read the play, what do you now understand by the name Godot? Why do you think Beckett chose the name for this mysterious figure?

2. Read pp. 18-22 of the text. What characteristics does Godot seem to have?

3. Estragon mistakes Pozzo for Godot (pp. 24-5), and on p. 33 and p. 42 Pozzo refers threateningly to what might happen if Vladimir and Estragon do not stay for their appointment. Say how far you agree with the idea that Pozzo is Godot.

4. How far do you agree with the view that *Waiting for Godot* is not primarily a play about Godot but about waiting and what people do while they are waiting?

5. 'Vladimir and Estragon are waiting for the end; "the end" is given a name: Godot.' (Colin Duckworth).

    '. . . for us at least if not for the two men on the road, Godot has become a concept – an idea of promise and expectation – of that for which people aware of the absence of coherent meaning in their lives wait in the hope that it will restore significance to their existence.'
    (Lawrence Graver)

    'There is no evidence that Godot exists as an objective reality outside the tramps' consciousness.'
    (Colin Duckworth)

    Discuss these views of Godot and then present the view of Godot that you have arrived at.

Characterisation

In the Comprehension section, many questions have already been asked about characterisation. Here the intention is to consider the characters not only in themselves but as embodiments of Beckett's vision of life, since the 'meaning' of the play, as Duckworth points out, is inseparable from the 'meaning' of the characters.

1. Vladimir and Estragon are sometimes said to have a certain anonymity. What does this derive from?

2. What evidence is there that they are placed in a situation beyond their understanding and what does this tell us about the human condition?

3. What differences do you observe between Vladimir and Estragon? For example, which is the more intellectual, which the more physical?

4. Vladimir and Estragon have been said to represent a Cartesian dualism between mind and body (Beckett studied Descartes and the Belgian Cartesian Geulincx). Giving reasons for your answer, say whether you find this way of approaching the play through a set of philosophical ideas illuminating. Does the idea of a body/mind dualism help in understanding the characters of Vladimir and Estragon and what they represent?

5. Discuss Vladimir and Estragon as clowns in the tradition of Chaplin, Laurel and Hardy and Buster Keaton. What do the characters contribute to the meaning of the play when seen in this way?

6. Why are Vladimir and Estragon so mutually dependent? What keeps them together? In presenting them as dependent on each other, what is Beckett saying about the human condition?

7. Beckett used the term 'pseudocouple' to refer to a pair of characters in one of his novels. To what extent can we view Vladimir and Estragon as a 'pseudocouple'?

8. Colin Duckworth challenges the view of some writers that Vladimir and Estragon are 'not really persons' by listing various adjectives to describe each of them. Complete the following two sentences by choosing from the list of adjectives.

a) Vladimir is the more . . .

b) Estragon is the more . . .

> active   acutely anguished   altruistic   analytical
> animal   articulate   bitter   buoyant   childish
> cultured   dependent   dignified   egotistic   forgetful
> impatient   instinctual   intelligent   lethargic
> obstinate   philosophical   protective   sensitive
> spontaneous   strong-willed   sulky   victimised

9. Write an essay on the characters of Vladimir and Estragon

a) as individuals;

b) as a couple.

10. Beckett and Roger Blin (the first director of *Waiting for Godot*) saw Pozzo 'as an English gentleman farmer, carrying a case of wine bottles, wearing a beautiful necktie, bowler hat and gleaming leather riding boots'. He is, then, a very impressive, very commanding figure. Quote evidence in the text of Act 1 which indicates the role of Pozzo as landowner, master, even tyrant.

11. On p. 36 Pozzo says that he owes his wealth to chance. Referring to Lucky, he says: 'Remark that I might just as well have been in his shoes and he in mine. If chance had not willed otherwise.' What might be the implications of this remark?

12. Lucky, the stage directions tell us, sags and straightens 'with the rhythm of one sleeping on his feet'. What might this symbolise in relation to his character and social situation?

13. Lucky has a running sore on his neck. What might this symbolise?

14. Various references suggest that Lucky has dog-like qualities. Find any such references and say what they suggest about Lucky.

15. Why should Pozzo be in raptures about the way Estragon addresses Lucky (p. 30)?

16. How is the beginning of the degeneration of a) Pozzo and b) Lucky already shown in Act 1?

A C T I V I T I E S

17. Giving reasons for your decisions, say which of the following adjectives would be appropriate and which inappropriate to a description of the Pozzo of Act 1:

> affected   authoritarian   condescending   harsh
> humble   humorous   inhuman   patient   pompous
> sincere   sympathetic   understanding

18. In Act 2 we hear Pozzo's cries of 'Help!', 'Pity!' and 'Don't leave me!' What is the significance of these cries in relation to important themes in the play?

19. In what ways have Pozzo and Lucky declined in Act 2 and what is the significance of this degeneration?

20. Pozzo refers to waking up one fine day and finding himself blind. He says he wonders sometimes if he is not still asleep. In what way does this connect him with Vladimir and Estragon and what is the significance of his remark in relation to one of the major themes of the play?

21. Write an essay on Pozzo and Lucky a) as individuals; b) as a couple.

22. Compare and contrast the relationship between Vladimir and Estragon with that between Pozzo and Lucky.

Structure and Theatrical Technique

1. In 1975 Beckett directed *Waiting for Godot* for the Schiller Theatre in Berlin. His director's notes are collected in a notebook, the *Regiebuch*, which is kept in the Beckett Archives in the library of Reading University. His director's notebook opens with the division of the play into eleven sections comprising eleven complete scenic units. He divided Act 1 into six sections and Act 2 into five sections, as follows:

    - A1 pp. 5-11   (to 'bloody ignorant apes')
    - A2 pp. 11-23   (to 'Like to finish it?')
    - A3 pp. 23-32   (to 'Let's go')
    - A4 pp. 32-45   (to 'my memory is defective')
    - A5 pp. 45-59   ('Pig! Yip! Adieu')
    - A6 pp. 59-67   (to the end of the first act)
    - B1 pp. 89-100   (to 'Exactly')
    - B2 pp. 100-15   (to 'Pity! On me!')
    - B3 pp. 115-23   (to 'We are men')
    - B4 pp. 123-33   (to 'it's night once more')
    - B5 pp. 133-39   (to the end of Act 2).

    Study the play in the light of Beckett's divisions and suggest why he divided the play in this way.

ACTIVITIES

2. According to Lawrence Graver, 'the basic structural unit of the play . . . is a self-contained routine or ritual.' Let us examine some of these units to establish their basic pattern. Read the opening of the play and answer the following questions:

    a) What is Estragon doing?
    b) What happens after the first pantomime?
    c) What happens in the next pantomime? And in the third?
    d) What follows the second pantomime? What follows the third?

3. We can say, then, that each of these 'units' starts with a pantomime followed normally by a moment of stillness in which the action is frozen into a tableau, followed by a dialogue containing comic and philosophical elements. In the first unit, for example, Vladimir interprets 'Nothing to be done' and 'the last moment' in ways not intended by Estragon. In the second unit, we have the pantomime of Vladimir taking off his hat and peering into it while Estragon examines his toes, followed by a tableau and silence, followed by Vladimir's musings on the two thieves. The third unit begins with the pantomime of Estragon limping first to the extreme left then to the extreme right, each time gazing into the distance, while Vladimir watches and then picks up Estragon's boot, peers into it and drops it with disgust. In two moments of stillness which follow, Estragon stands first with his back to the audience then facing the audience directly. Then follows the introduction of the theme of waiting for Godot, marked by a pause, a moment of silence and stillness, followed by the discussion of the tree and whether they have come to the right place on the right day.

A C T I V I T I E S

a) Study the dialogue of the third unit mentioned above, from Estragon: *'Charming spot'*. How does Beckett here subvert the audience's confidence in its ability to distinguish between illusion and reality?

b) Find two other 'units' in Act 1 which follow the pattern of pantomime and tableau followed by speech.

c) What is the dramatic function of the pantomime and tableau in each of your examples and what is the subsequent dialogue in each about?

4. Read Act 1 from the beginning to the entrance of Pozzo and Lucky, and answer the following questions:

a) What are the main subdivisions in this section of the text ?

b) Note the first time that the waiting for Godot is mentioned, and Estragon's reaction to the situation.

c) What do the tramps do to pass the time while waiting?

d) What is the keynote of the discussion about Godot?

e) What do the tramps say about their relationship with Godot?

f) What part is played by food in this section of the play?

5. Read Act 2 from the beginning to the entry of Pozzo and Lucky, and answer the following questions:

a) What are the main subdivisions of this section of Act 2?

b) What is Vladimir's song about and what is its structure?

c) When is the first reference to the idea of waiting for Godot in this act? What is Estragon's reaction?

d) What is the dramatic effect of the passage about the dead voices?

A C T I V I T I E S

   e) What part is played by food in this section of Act 2? What has changed since Act 1?

   f) Describe the routine with the hats. Do you find it amusing? Why/ why not?

   g) What is the purpose and effect of the game of imitating Pozzo and Lucky?

   h) What do the tramps do to pass time in this section? Describe their various activities.

   i) How many references to 'waiting for Godot' can you find in this section?

6. In what ways are Vladimir and Estragon's 'routines' in Act 2 different from those in Act 1? What might be the significance of the difference(s)?

7. What other similarities and differences do you notice in the two sequences from Acts 1 and 2 you have been studying? Do you find the similarities or the differences more striking? Give reasons for your answer.

8. Now compare the scenes with Pozzo and Lucky in Acts 1 and 2, and answer the following questions:

   a) How have Pozzo and Lucky changed in Act 2?

   b) What differences are there in the actions of the two scenes?

   c) Describe the importance of Lucky's monologue in Act 1.

   d) If Lucky's monologue is the central element of the Pozzo/Lucky scene in Act 1, what would you consider to be the central element of the scene in Act 2?

   e) Which of the two scenes convey the greater sense of desperation? Give reasons for your answer.

   f) Are you more struck by the similarities or the differences between these two scenes? Give reasons for your answer.

9. Compare the following scenes from Acts 1 and 2:

   a) from the exit of Pozzo and Lucky to the entry of the boy;

   b) from the entrance of the boy to his exit;

   c) from the exit of the boy to the end of the act.

   Note any similarities or differences between the equivalent scenes in each act and, giving reasons for your answer, say which you find more striking, the similarities or the differences.

10. Having compared the various scenes of Acts 1 and 2, a) how would you say Act 2 differs from Act 1 and b) what conclusions do you come to about the structure of the play?

11. In what ways do the following reflect the structure of the whole play:

   a) Vladimir's song at the beginning of Act 2;

   b) the comic routine with the hats?

12. Why should Beckett have decided on two acts instead of one or three or five?

13. How might you represent the structure of *Waiting for Godot* in a diagram?

14. The structure has been described as being circular; as a series of links in a chain; as a downward spiral. Comment on each of these possibilities and decide which of them you consider the most appropriate, giving reasons for your choice.

15. Ruby Cohn, one of Beckett's most famous critics, wrote of the importance of 'doublets' in *Waiting for Godot*: two acts, two days, etc. In what other ways can we think of 'doublets' in the play?

ACTIVITIES

16. Colin Duckworth wrote: 'The structure of Godot thus achieves the rare quality of being both static and dynamic – a quality which is defined for us at the beginning of Act 2 with Vladimir's round-song.' Discuss this comment on the structure of *Waiting for Godot*.

17. '. . . there is a miraculous harmony between form and content' (Introduction). To what extent do you agree with this judgement?

18. The introduction refers to metatheatrical techniques, that is, moments in which a play 'draws attention to its own fictional status as a theatrical pretence' (Chris Baldick: *Concise Oxford Dictionary of Literary Terms*). One of these occurs on p. 12 of *Waiting for Godot*, when Estragon turns directly to the audience and says, 'Inspiring prospects.' Find other examples of such metatheatrical moments. Comment on each one, explaining why it is a metatheatrical moment. Why does Beckett introduce such moments into his play?

19. Discuss the role played by silence in the play. Choose two sections of the text to illustrate the dramatic use of silence in the play. How does Beckett make silence significant in your two examples?

20. In a performance of the play, what role would be played by

   a) setting;

   b) lighting;

   c) costume?

21. Given that inaction and silence play a dominant role in *Waiting for Godot*, what techniques does Beckett use to avoid boring his audience and to what extent do you think they are successful?

22. Discuss the problems of achieving a balance between seriousness and farce in performance of the play.

Language, Style and Symbolism

1. Examine the first dialogue between Vladimir and Estragon, from the beginning of the play to 'Hope deferred maketh the something sick, who said that?'

   a) What is the general tone and style of the dialogue?

   b) What serious undertones are suggested, and how?

2. Comment on two further sequences of dialogue between Vladimir and Estragon, illustrating how banal conversation can acquire cosmic undertones.

3. Read carefully the sequence of dialogue from *Estragon: 'What about hanging ourselves?'* to *Vladimir: 'I think so too.' Silence.* (pp. 16-19) Such sequences suggest the music-hall dialogue of a comic double act. What gives the dialogue that quality and what suggests seriousness beneath the fooling?

4. Find and comment on another passage with this quality of music-hall dialogue.

5. Read the passage in which Vladimir and Estragon talk about 'all the dead voices' (pp. 96-7). Comment on its style and its emotional effect on reader or audience.

6. Comment on the style of Pozzo's language, focusing on:

   a) the different ways he talks a) to Lucky and b) to Vladimir and Estragon;

   b) the pompousness of his manner of speaking;

   c) any contrast between his language in Act 1 and in Act 2;

   d) his 'disquisitions' on the tears of the world (p. 37), on night (pp. 43-4), and on time (pp. 132-3).

7. Certain moments, such as the passage about the dead voices or Pozzo's speech on time stand out from the general style of the play. Other such passages would be Lucky's monologue and Vladimir's final long speech (p. 134). What is the overall effect of such moments on the tone of the play and on our response to the situation presented in the play?

8. Choose and comment on two examples of Beckett's use of vulgar language.

9. Discuss the variety of styles used in the play and choose three examples to show how and for what purposes Beckett deliberately uses contrasting styles.

10. Walter Asmus talked about the play's 'structure of repetitions'. Choose three examples of the use of repetition and comment on their effect. What repetitions become more insistent in Act 2?

11. Beckett presents an absurd universe. Discuss the way he uses language to achieve this sense of absurdity.

12. Though Beckett saw language as an inadequate way of conveying true knowledge of reality, it remains the only instrument we have with which to make the attempt. Choose two passages to illustrate the breakdown of language as the characters try to discuss their situation.

13. *Waiting for Godot* has attracted many allegorical and symbolic interpretations. Define the difference between allegory and symbolism.

14. Allegorical interpretations of *Waiting for Godot* are restricting and reductive, and Beckett himself spoke of the habit critics have of seeing 'symbols where none intended'. This was disingenuous of him, since he would know as well as anyone that symbols are not merely a matter of conscious intentions. Comment on the following uses of symbolism by completing the grid.

Symbol	Possible significance
Estragon's feet/Vladimir's urinary problems	
The verbal routines and rituals performed by Vladimir and Estragon	
The removing and replacing of hats	
The rope tying Pozzo and Lucky together	
Lucky's speech	
Vladimir's round-song	
The three hats for two heads routine	
The 'all fall down' sequence in Act 2	
Pozzo's blindness/Lucky's dumbness	
Pozzo's loss of his pipe, vaporiser and watch	

15. Comment on any other examples of symbolism you can find in the play.

ACTIVITIES

General Questions

1. Colin Duckworth lists a number of Beckett's preoccupations and beliefs. Some of these are listed below. Comment on the relevance of each to *Waiting for Godot*.

   • 'definition of Self depends on memory and this is imprecise';

   • 'our everyday existence is of doubtful reality';

   • 'words give thoughts their existence, and are therefore the only defence against being plunged into Nothingness . . . , the Void . . . of silence and timelessness';

   • 'if a god exists, it is a malevolent entity, demanding and capricious';

   • 'earthly life is a punishment for an unknown crime, perhaps the crime of being born'.

2. 'Nothing to be done.' To what extent does the play confirm the validity of its opening line?

3. Beckett called his play 'a tragicomedy in two acts'.

   a) What elements of the tragic and of the comic do you find in the play?

   b) To what extent are the tragic and the comic integrated in the play?

4. Estragon says of his carrot that the more you eat the worse it gets. In the play as a whole discuss whether life gets worse or better, or stays the same.

5. Discuss the vision of life presented by *Waiting for Godot*, commenting on how successful you feel Beckett is in communicating that vision.

Notes

NOTES

NOTES

Titles in the same series

Samuel Beckett
WAITING FOR GODOT

Joseph Conrad
HEART OF DARKNESS

Charles Dickens
A CHRISTMAS CAROL

Dickens, Stevenson *et al.*
SHORT STORIES

Arthur Conan Doyle *et al.*
DETECTIVE STORIES

F. Scott Fitzgerald
THE GREAT GATSBY

Ford Madox Ford
THE GOOD SOLDIER

E. M. Forster
A PASSAGE TO INDIA
A ROOM WITH A VIEW

N. Gordimer, C. Achebe *et al.*
FOUR CONTINENTS

Aldous Huxley
BRAVE NEW WORLD

Henry James
THE TURN OF THE SCREW

James Joyce
DUBLINERS
A selection from DUBLINERS
A PORTRAIT OF THE ARTIST
  AS A YOUNG MAN

R. Kipling *et al.*
EMPIRE TALES

D. H. Lawrence
THE FOX

Katherine Mansfield
SEVEN SHORT STORIES

John Osborne
LOOK BACK IN ANGER

Edgar Allan Poe
SELECTED STORIES

Edgar Allan Poe
and H. G. Wells
THE MARVELLOUS AND
  THE STRANGE

George Bernard Shaw
PYGMALION

Mary Shelley
FRANKENSTEIN

Robert Louis Stevenson
THE STRANGE CASE OF
  DR JEKYLL AND MR HYDE
  and Other Stories

Oscar Wilde
THE IMPORTANCE OF BEING
  EARNEST
THE PICTURE OF DORIAN
  GRAY
SHORT STORIES

Virginia Woolf
MRS DALLOWAY
TO THE LIGHTHOUSE